*To the memory of my parents,
whose godly lives were a powerful influence
in bringing all four of their children
to new life in Christ*

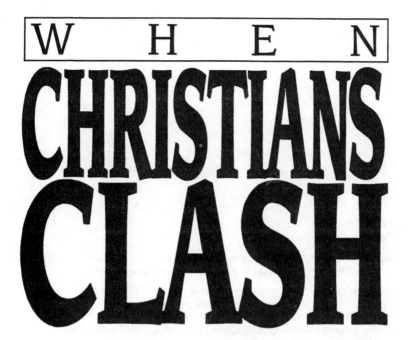

W H E N
CHRISTIANS
CLASH

How to Prevent & Resolve the Pain of Conflict

Horace L. Fenton, Jr.

INTERVARSITY PRESS
DOWNERS GROVE, ILLINOIS 60515

InterVarsity Press is the book-publishing division of InterVarsity Christian Fellowship, a student movement active on campus at hundreds of universities, colleges and schools of nursing. For information about local and regional activities, write Public Relations Dept., InterVarsity Christian Fellowship, 6400 Schroeder Rd., P.O. Box 7895, Madison, WI 53707-7895.

Distributed in Canada through InterVarsity Press, 860 Denison St., Unit 3, Markham, Ontario L3R 4H1, Canada.

Scripture quotations, unless otherwise noted, are from the Holy Bible: New International Version. © 1978 by the New York International Bible Society. Used by permission of Zondervan Bible Publishers.

Cover illustration: Joe DeVelasco

Edited by Dave and Neta Jackson

ISBN 0-8308-1701-8

Printed in the United States of America

Library of Congress Cataloging in Publication Data

Fenton, Horace L.
    When Christians clash.

    1. Church controversies.   2. Interpersonal
relations—Religious aspects—Christianity.
I. Title.
BV652.9.F46   1987   250   87-29402
ISBN 0-8308-1701-8

16	15	14	13	12	11	10	9	8	7	6	5	4	3	2	1
99	98	97	96	95	94	93	92	91	90	89	88	87			

Preface

You don't have to be a Christian very long before you discover that the members of your new family in Christ don't always get along well with each other.

Perhaps that should be no great surprise to any of us. After all, in our blood families, brothers and sisters often find themselves in violent disagreement. And parents and children not only disagree, but sometimes the arguments leave long-lasting scars. So why should we think it strange if our spiritual family, into which we're born through faith in Christ, should also have fights? After all, we didn't stop being human when we became Christians, and all humans seem prone to disagree with those closest to them and even to escalate those conflicts into lethal battles.

Yet somehow, we can't fully adjust to watching Christians clash, or to see them inflict serious wounds on each other in the process of defending a particular point of view. And even though, as Joyce

Huggett points out in her helpful book *Creative Conflict* (InterVarsity Press, 1984), there is such a thing as profiting from and even making friends of conflict, most of us have difficulty in coming to terms with civil war, especially within the bonds of what the "street Christians" of the 1960s called God's Forever Family. If God can reconcile us to himself—and there is no gulf wider than the chasm between a sinful people and a holy God—can he not reconcile his children to one another?

Believers ought to be deeply concerned about the animosities, antagonisms and bitter conflicts so prevalent within the family of God. For what can unbelievers think of us when, as Joe Bayly suggested, our theme song seems to be: "The strife is o'er, the battle done. Our church has split, and our side won"? The number of broken homes within the membership of evangelical churches, the tragic divisions within local congregations, and the lack of love which so frequently characterizes doctrinal disputes within denominations—these are all too evident throughout the Christian church, and there is little likelihood of overstating them.

What is likely, however, is that we'll be paralyzed by the sheer weight of these situations because we don't know where to take hold of them. So we substitute lamentation for prayer, and indulge in hand-wringing instead of seeking the basic principles which God has given in his Word to help us find the road to peace.

This book represents one Christian's attempt to point out some of the guidelines revealed in Scripture which show us the way toward peace and unity. My own thinking about what to do when Christians clash grew out of a study I made some years ago of the book of Acts. I had been through this wonderful history of the early church many times before, but this time, as I prepared a series of messages for use in churches and Bible conferences, I saw Acts in a new way.

For here were the first-century Christians struggling with differences in viewpoint, interpretation and doctrinal beliefs—not to mention personality conflicts and centuries-old tensions between Jews and Gentiles—which threatened again and again to blow the fledgling church apart. The wonderful unity which had characterized Christ's disciples on the day of Pentecost and which they all recognized was a precious gift of God, seemed under constant attack.

Yet somehow, by the grace of God and through the wisdom given to them by the Holy Spirit, these first-century believers found a way not only to differ with each other in love (in itself no small thing!), but also, on many occasions, to reconcile their differences or to learn to live above them. Friends and co-workers were saved from needless conflict; local churches were spared the awful trauma of splinterings and schisms; Satan's persistent efforts to divide and corrupt the body of Christ were roundly resisted.

"How did they do it?" I found myself asking. So I went back to my study of Acts and to other biblical accounts in the Old and New Testaments in which conflict threatened the family of God. There I saw some things I hadn't seen before. When I found some answers which helped me to deal with several tense situations in my own corner of the church, I felt an obligation to share with other Christians the lessons I was learning.

My fifty-two years of service in the gospel has made me painfully aware of how much twentieth-century believers need help restoring unity to their relationships and ministries. I have, therefore, included many illustrations from my own personal experience. (For obvious reasons, fictitious names have been given to most of the participants. In a few cases, the story told includes details drawn, not from this particular instance, but from similar cases I have known.)

I was greatly encouraged when InterVarsity Press editors confirmed my conviction that the contemporary church needs all the help it can get in the area of conflict resolution. The editors helped me to believe that my own study of Scripture and experience in the church both at home and abroad would be helpful to many who share my concern about the lack of unity in many parts of the church of Christ today. And so, with many reservations about my own competence for such a task, but with an inner compulsion that whatever I could do, with God's help I ought to do, I began work on this book.

That was too many years ago! While the Lord has graciously encouraged me again and again in the task, my progress on the manuscript has been slow. Nevertheless, my experience through these years with Andrew Le Peau, managing editor of InterVarsity Press, and other members of the IVP staff has convinced me that an aspiring writer could hope for no greater blessing than a sympathetic publisher and an editor whose patience is matched only by his ability to challenge, correct and encourage his protégé. I also have much reason to be grateful for the helpful suggestions of David and Neta Jackson, and for their skilled editing of the text. The Lord has truly answered the prayers of friends who have wished that I might have expert help along these lines.

There are, of course, others who have greatly encouraged me when I have been tempted to give up on the whole project. My wife who has shared my life and my ministry for fifty-two years, has consistently shown her deep interest in this assignment, without adding to my sense of guilt over my slowness in completing it. My sister, Mildred, graciously offered her expert help in the typing and retyping of the manuscript, just at the time when I was thoroughly disheartened over my own hunt-and-peck approach to getting this part of the task done.

I would be terribly remiss if I did not also express my heartfelt thanks to the wonderful friends God has given me among the membership of the First Presbyterian Church of Bethlehem, Pennsylvania, where I have been privileged to serve during the past ten years. I have known many fine churches in the course of my ministry, but I have never known one more characterized by love for Christ and for each other. Their readiness to affirm any service I have been able to do for my Lord and for them has been a source of great encouragement to me. Knowing that I have been struggling to finish this particular manuscript over a period of years, they have again and again expressed their interest in the progress I was making, and indeed have lovingly held me to account for keeping at it. It has been a source of unspeakable joy to spend the latter years of my ministry in an atmosphere such as this, and I find myself thanking the Lord again and again for the way these choice brothers and sisters have enriched my life, and encouraged me to be and do my best for the Lord.

Every Christian sooner or later becomes aware that at our best we are products of all the gracious influences the Lord has brought to bear on our lives. Sometimes when I lie awake at night, I enjoy making a mental list of the many people who have made a contribution, small or large, to my life and service for Jesus Christ. The list is in constant need of updating, and it seems to be forever extending itself. This little exercise of thanksgiving has an overwhelming effect on me at times, producing waves of both gratitude and humility, and creating in me an awesome sense of responsibility, if not to pay the debt I owe, at least to demonstrate that I am aware of it.

I have finished this task, with relief and gratitude, gladly committing its helpfulness to others into the hands of our sovereign God. I have no way of knowing whether it is the last book I shall be permitted to write, but I marvel at the grace of God in allowing me to bring this manuscript to completion. There are a number of other themes on which I should like to write, dealing with lessons the Lord has patiently taught me through the years. But my times, like yours, are in his hands, and neither you nor I would have it otherwise. As I await this leading, I find great joy in praying a brief prayer which I came across a few years ago: "Lord, give me work while life shall last, and life, 'til work is done."

Horace L. Fenton, Jr.

1

A Word
for the
Road

DON'T QUARREL ON THE WAY!"

How often anxious parents say this to their lively offspring as the family starts out on a long trip! Mom and Dad are well aware that a tiresome journey lies ahead, and the space in which the youngsters are confined will seem smaller and smaller as the tedious hours drag by. So the parents, already weary from preparing for the trip, give a stern warning in the vain hope that it will have some pacifying effect.

But this admonition has a long history. When the sons of Jacob arrived in Egypt seeking relief from the drought and famine which had ravaged their homeland, they hadn't expected to find their long-lost brother Joseph—alive, and in a position of great honor and responsibility second only to the Pharaoh. Years before in a fit of jealousy they had sold their younger brother into slavery. When Joseph made himself known to his startled brothers, they realized that their lives were in his hands. Undoubtedly they feared the worst.

To their great surprise, Joseph offered them complete forgiveness. This godly man, whom they had hated passionately, urged them to return to their homeland and bring back their father, so that the reunited family could enjoy the riches of Egypt.

But as they were about to leave on their long journey, Joseph, knowing his brothers well, warned: "Don't quarrel on the way!" (Gen 45:24).

The story of the people of God shows ample need for many similar warnings. Tired from the long pilgrimage, they have often taken out their frustrations on each other. The children of Israel complaining in the desert . . . Saul pursuing David . . . tension between Jewish and Gentile Christians . . . splintering into denominations . . . . It was so easy to forget relationships in such times and to give free rein to attitudes and actions which spoiled the journey for everyone.

You don't have to be a church historian, however, to be aware that in our own times the church has often been grievously wounded by interfamily quarrels. Other relationships have been marred by labor-management strife, breaking of long-standing friendships, our sorry record in the divorce courts, and repeated conflicts and dissension.

It's not hard to believe that the still small voice of God has often been speaking these age-old words, "Don't quarrel on the way!" That voice is not denying for a moment that we have an Enemy with whom we are called to make war, but it does insist that we remember who that Enemy is, and that we direct our fire at Satan, not at our brothers and sisters in Christ.

The Enemy at Work

Some of the most wonderful years of my life were spent in Costa Rica. I came to love the people, their language and culture, and the beauty of the land. After an absence of some years, I had the privilege of going back for visits in 1984 and 1986.

Even as I returned to that lovely country, I was reminded of Thomas Wolfe's words that "you can't go home again!" I knew I couldn't expect things to be as they had been when I lived there, and that I would find many things different from my golden-hued memories.

I indeed found the changes I had anticipated, plus many that I hadn't expected. Some of these were wonderful—the giant steps the church had taken toward spiritual maturity in my absence; the miraculous numerical growth of the church; and many new groups springing up in what I had thought was barren soil. Everywhere the leadership was in the hands of competent national believers, and under them the work had been thriving to a degree many of us old-time missionaries had prayed for but hadn't expected to see in our lifetime. There was abundant reason for praising God.

But there were other changes that were not so encouraging. In earlier days my Latin brothers and sisters had exhibited a wonderful measure of unity in Christ when, as a beleaguered minority, they had nobly resisted the efforts of the Enemy to divide them. They had stood shoulder to shoulder, regardless of the widely varied denominational origins from which those little groups had sprung.

They had refused to allow the winds of heretical doctrine or the pressure of recruiters from ecumenically minded organizations to separate them from their fellow believers. They had largely rejected pettiness, competition and self-protection which had threatened to sow seeds of dissension in their Christian groups. They had refused to let charismatic issues divide them from one another, and they had rejected the party labels which have been so divisive in North American evangelical Christianity. If they failed to maintain complete unity in the family of God, they certainly had a measure of it that I had never experienced in my early days as a denominational pastor in the United States.

But in these recent visits I noted disturbing changes. The constant political ferment, the economic and social pressures, the battles over secondary doctrinal differences and other tensions now seemed to be taking their toll. Large and small issues now took on life-and-death significance, and with Christians sorely divided among themselves over what or whom to support.

Some, for instance, were supporters of the Sandinista revolution in Nicaragua, seeing it as consistent with the trend toward more freedom and less oppression; others denounced its communist inspiration. The advent of "liberation theology" (or the many different "liberation theologies") divided Christians along many lines. In a Third World country with few natural resources, utterly dependent on what their products could be sold for, there was a sense of helplessness and dissatisfaction with their situation. A brilliant ex-president of Costa Rica once told a group of us, "Better for us than all the U.S. foreign aid would be a readiness, on the part of your country, to pay fifteen cents per pound more for coffee!"

As Christians disagreed on gut-level political issues, I saw that part of their self-defense was to accuse those they disagreed with of suspicious theology. "How can you be a Christian and support that?" What the Adversary had not been able to accomplish in earlier times was now coming to pass before our eyes—bitter conflicts in local churches, competitiveness among larger groups, Christians taking sides against each other in ways that shattered long-term relationships.

It was a sobering experience which moved me to pray for the unity of Christ's body in Latin America and throughout the world.

It seemed that I could hear again and again the tender voice of a deeply aggrieved Father crying out to his fractious children, "You're on the road to glory: In the name of Christ, don't quarrel on the way!"

But do we hear the pleading of God and apply it to our family relationships, our church fellowships or even to our day-by-day conflicts with our fellow Christians? I ask myself, "Must we always be quibbling, quarreling children who, weary of the long journey, make life miserable for ourselves and for others, all the while breaking the heart of God by our acknowledged disunity?"

John Stott is on target when in his book, *Involvement: Being a Responsible Christian in a Non-Christian Society*, he reminds us that

> God's call to us is not only to "preach peace" and to "make peace," but also to embody it. For his purpose, through the work of his Son and his Spirit, is to create a new reconciled society in which no curtains, walls, or barriers are tolerated, and in which the divisive influences of race, nationality, rank, and sex have been destroyed. He means his Church to be a sign of his Kingdom, that is a model of what human community looks like when it comes under his rule of righteousness and peace. An authentic Kingdom community will then challenge the value system of the secular community and offer a viable alternative. We can hardly call the world to peace while the Church falls short of being the reconciled community God intends it to be. If charity begins at home, so does reconciliation . . . . The influence for peace of communities of peace is inestimable.

Is this an unattainable ideal, which ultimately serves not to challenge us, but to frustrate and mock us? Is there any reason to hope that in a world of bitter strife, with even Christians warring against each other, we can experience the unity which Christ intended for his followers?

Against such seeming evidence to the contrary, I dare to believe that there is, or I would not have written this book. My hope (which I have to confess is not always constant) is based on two significant factors, which I want to state briefly here and then to expound more fully in the remaining chapters of the book.

Grounds for Hope

1. The experience of God's people. Granted, experience is not always a safe guide. Like the sword of the Spirit, it is a two-edged instrument. One can draw seemingly contradictory conclusions from the church's past experiences of dealing with internal conflicts. At times Christians have not been even as wise as the unregenerate people of the world in dealing with their disagreements. But the tragic events of the past may teach us how to handle such situations better than some of our forefathers did.

Fortunately, there is another side to the story—one which offers us hope that God's people can be peacemakers in both our personal relationships and in our corporate dealings. In my own study of the biblical incidents which we shall consider in this book, I have been given hope again and again by Abraham, Peter, Paul, Euodia, Syntyche and others who sought God's wisdom in managing their conflicts and thus grew in their sense of unity as members of God's redeemed family. The Lord encourages us by their examples to believe that he can enable us to experience such unity in our own daily pilgrimage.

These people were not sinless saints. They were just as vulnerable as we are to Satan's strategy of disunity. Like us, they were goaded by their old natures into hasty words which couldn't be recalled; they made unkind judgments and held prejudiced opinions; they were involved in bitter controversy. They didn't always handle their conflicts well, nor did they consistently esteem God's gift of unity as highly as they should have.

But as we look at certain incidents in their lives, we learn that these "frail children of dust, and feeble as frail" sometimes allowed the Spirit of God to turn them away from their bickering with one another and enabled them to settle their differences. Their unity in the Lord became a precious reality, not to be lightly cast aside as a result of their quarreling on the way.

In studying these stories, I have discovered no sure-fire formula for preserving the peace and unity of the church. But I have had fresh assurance that our conflicts, small and large, can be resolved to the glory of God. And I dare to pray that the light of that assurance may shine on the lives of some of my fellow Christians who find themselves embroiled in unity-destroying controversy with others who also belong to the family of God.

2. The basis of God's appeal to us. When Joseph charged his brothers not to quarrel on the way, his words carried a note of authority because of what he had already done for them. The memory of his gracious treatment of them was fresh in their minds. Nothing that they might quarrel about would seem of any consequence compared to the evil way they had treated him, yet he had fully and freely forgiven them for all their actions. How then, having tasted the joys of reconciliation with him, dared they tolerate new friction among themselves?

Moreover, the background of his exhortation was the gracious promise he had made concerning their future. To be sure, they had a long and wearisome round trip ahead, not without great danger. But at the end of it all, they and their father would be well provided for. They would be accompanied on their trip by the memory of Joseph's goodness and mercy, and when their pilgrimage was ended, they would dwell with their brother in the land where he would share his abundance with them. In the light of such a prospect, it made no sense whatever that by quarreling among themselves on the way they should in any way postpone or prevent their arrival in the land Joseph had promised them.

But Someone who is greater than Joseph speaks to us! It is the God who yearns over us when we reject his love, and who forgives all our rebellion and waywardness. He pleads with us to forget our feuding with one another in his family as we rejoice in his grace toward us and journey toward our eternal home with him.

Whatever differences we have with other brothers and sisters in Christ, we are, above all else, members of the same family, having this in common—all of us need the forgiving grace of God and the fellowship of each other. Meanwhile, the forgiveness he has so freely given us must be extended to each other. Is it not therefore reasonable that he who at such cost reconciled us to himself should insist that day by day we be reconciled to each other? And how do we dare call him "Lord, Lord," if in our interpersonal relationships we refuse to do what he commands?

No one pretends that it will be easy. There is no painless formula for success in this difficult area. Settling the controversies we shall be considering did not come to pass easily, nor was peace in the family bought at bargain-basement prices. But these disputes were resolved, and if we are truly open to learn from the experience of those who have gone before us, there is hope that we too shall enjoy the blessing of God and the fellowship of those who are on the journey with us.

2

A Rift between Relatives

GOT TO KNOW Ted and Frances well in one of the first churches I pastored. She had grown up in the church. He, a relatively late arrival, was active along with her in the thriving young adults' group. I watched their romance develop and was delighted when they asked me to officiate at their wedding.

For me, that wedding was a special event. Their love for each other seemed to be of a mature sort, as was their obvious commitment to the Lord. I had high hopes, not merely for the survival of their marriage, but for their great usefulness as servants of Christ in our church.

My high hopes were shattered a few years later when they came to my study to inform me of the shambles into which their marriage had fallen. The situation was made even more tragic by Ted's insistence that he saw no hope of continuing with Frances, while she desperately hoped that some kind of miracle could yet save their marriage. She seemed genuinely willing to face up to her own failure in maintaining a relationship. But Ted, disclaiming any culpability, seemed satisfied to say that he was no longer in love with her, and that he was sure that divorce was the only way out.

At this point, the faith in God which they had ardently professed at the time of their wedding seemed inoperative. Frances felt that her prayers had been utterly ineffective, and Ted admittedly had drifted away from the warm relationship with Christ he had once enjoyed.

As they launched their charges and countercharges against each other, I heard what sounded like the death knell of my idealism about their future together. That was some years ago, but I'm no less shocked by such interviews today, and they seem to be taking place more frequently than ever before.

But family conflict in the church isn't limited to unhappy husbands and wives. Deborah and Nancy are sisters. Each claims a relationship to Christ. Both worship in the same church. But as a result of a long, bitter family feud, they do not speak to one another—in church or out.

Myrna, a single parent, was estranged from her Jewish parents and hadn't seen them in seven years, even though they lived in the same city. Only after Myrna was killed in a tragic accident did her pastor and a church counselor make contact with the family—and discovered caring and hurting parents. The family invited church members to the funeral. The church invited the family to a memorial service, where the parents learned for the first time what had been happening in their daughter's life for the last seven years. A measure of reconciliation and resolution took place—all too late for Myrna.

When we are involved in a family rift, we tend to justify our case:

"You don't understand; he's impossible to live with"; "No matter what I do she's not satisfied"; "My parents never listen to me"; "Forgive him? He doesn't think he's done anything wrong!"

We often find it easier to love those outside our family circle than to love those to whom we are intimately related.

The church is the family of God, and as members within it we are brothers and sisters in Christ. Natural families within the church are also brothers and sisters in Christ, and what happens to them affects all of us. Family strife is always an ugly thing, and something inside us tells us that it's utterly contrary to what God meant to be.

How does our Christian faith relate to conflict between those who are related to each other? Does the Bible offer us any help in confronting such sad experiences?

Way Back at the Beginning

There's nothing new about domestic conflict. It dates back to the dispute between Cain and Abel in the early days of human history. Abel, a shepherd, brought a blood sacrifice to the Lord. Cain, a farmer, brought an offering of vegetables. "The LORD looked with favor on Abel and his offering, but on Cain and his offering he did not look with favor. So Cain was very angry . . ." (Gen 4:4-5). In a jealous rage, Cain lured his brother into a field, attacked and killed him.

This story, which follows so closely on the heels of Papa Adam's and Mama Eve's disobedience and the entrance of sin into the world, is direct evidence of the reality of the Fall, and makes it clear that such conflicts can end in utter disaster. We can be sure that God was wounded in heart by the conflict of these brothers, even before its tragic end-product proved to be murder.

A few chapters later we come to another biblical story of family strife, a dispute which cast a shadow over the relationship of

Abram and his nephew, Lot. But the encouraging thing in this story is that the dreadful potential of the domestic disagreement was not realized. The situation was neither ignored nor condoned as though it were of little significance. Instead, the dispute was resolved amicably. The record bears witness that even when ominous rifts in relationships threaten havoc, peace is still possible. Let's look at the story as it is given us in Genesis 13.

It all began with their herdsmen. Abram and Lot were what we might today call cattle barons. Their riches were not in bank accounts, but in the great herds of cattle they both possessed. Abram and Lot were wealthy—and that very fact became a flash point in their relationship.

As their flocks and herds multiplied, the competition for rich grazing land became intense, and the servants of the two men fell to quarreling over who should have the best pastures. The stage was set not only for bitter feeling between the ranch foremen, but between Abram and Lot themselves. And lurking in the shadows were the Canaanites and the Perizzites, who would gladly take advantage of the interfamily quarrel to despoil both of the conflicting parties.

Take the Initiative

It was Abram who saw the danger, and did something about it. *He took the initiative.* This exemplifies a principle which can help resolve many a domestic or church conflict in the twentieth century. Let's look at some of the lessons the ancient patriarch can teach us.

1. Anticipate the danger. Apparently the open conflict at this stage was limited to the hired help. There was as yet no break between the two relatives. Scripture doesn't say what Lot's response was. It's easy to imagine, however, that when Lot's herdsmen complained to their master about Abram's flocks crowding

out the choicest grazing land, Lot strode into the billowing no-
madic tent and confronted his uncle: "Look, Uncle Abram. Tell
your hired men to back off and give my herds some room. They're
pushing my men around out there."

Abram saw that this spark might at any moment set off a devastating firestorm. He realized that if the strife were permitted to
continue, it would affect the sound relationship which up till then
he and Lot had enjoyed. And he determined not to let that happen.
So he told his nephew, "Let's not have any quarreling between you
and me, or between your herdsmen and mine, for we are brothers"
(Gen 13:8).

Centuries later the apostle James wrote, "Consider what a great
forest is set on fire by a small spark" (Jas 3:5). I saw his words
dramatically illustrated a few years ago.

At that time I was speaking at a retreat sponsored by Mission
Aviation Fellowship for its furloughed and stateside personnel. We
were on a college campus in central California, and the setting was
one of rare beauty. Early one evening we gathered in the audito-
rium for a film. Suddenly, all the lights in the building went out.
After waiting a reasonable time for the power to come back on,
we were advised to leave the building. We groped our way out of
the darkness into the gathering twilight outdoors.

There we were confronted by a lurid red sky and the leaping
flames of a forest fire only a few miles away. As we watched, the
conflagration seemed to move inexorably in our direction. The
crackling of the flames was almost thunderous, and we stood
transfixed as acres of beautiful forest were devoured in spite of the
efforts of firefighters to extinguish the flames both from airplanes
and on the ground.

The spectacle was awe-inspiring, and at the same time far more
terrifying than all the pictures I had seen of similar fires. We were
ordered to evacuate the campus without gathering up our posses-

sions in the dormitories. As we beat a retreat we got fleeting glimpses of the unbridled fury of the flames. Beautiful homes were engulfed and disappeared before our eyes, and we watched dumbstruck as millions of dollars worth of property was destroyed.

It all started, they told us, with a tiny spark—a carelessly discarded cigarette, a faulty electrical connection or something of the sort. Whatever the cause, the fire left scores of people homeless and vast tracts of forest land ravaged. If only someone had dealt with the situation while it was still a spark!

Abram smelled the smoke of a fire with potential for great damage. Even though it was a small spark, he knew that the time to deal with destructive conflict was *before* it got out of hand.

2. Move in promptly. Having spotted the danger, Abraham acted without delay. He knew better than to make light of the dispute, even in its early stages. Had he tried to minimize the significance of what was taking place, subsequent history might have been different. As Abram saw it, it was too easy for an argument between herdsmen to become a rift between relatives, with devastating consequences.

If no man is an island, as John Donne insisted, then no family quarrel is unimportant. It always carries with it the possibility of something more serious, especially if it is allowed to linger. Obviously, Abram cherished harmony in the home and in the brotherhood as being more important than winning a particular argument. "For we are brothers!" he said.

Recently, Fred came to see me about the imminent breakup of his marriage. His wife had moved out, taking half the furniture and all the picture albums, and was beginning divorce proceedings. Fred was really broken up. He didn't want a divorce and was struggling with feelings of rejection and self-justification.

"How long have you and your wife been having marital problems?" I asked.

He replied, "Ten years." Yet apparently only at this late stage had he sought counsel from anyone! Hindsight is invariably 20/20, but I wondered if Fred's story might have had a different ending if remedial action had been taken before petty skirmishes had become major battles.

3. Look for alternatives. Since "the land could not support them . . . for their possessions were so great" (Gen 13:6), it looked like someone had to win and someone had to lose.

As head of the family clan, Abram might easily have tried to settle the dispute to his own advantage, jealously protecting his own interests and insisting that preferential consideration be given to his own concerns. He might have tried to debate the issue with his nephew or remind Lot of the respect he owed his uncle. He might have counted on the numerical superiority of his forces to insure getting his own way. To do any of these things would be natural enough, given the tendency of all of us to protect what we feel is rightly ours at whatever cost.

In doing so, however, Abram might have won the battle and lost the war. That's always a danger in our interpersonal conflicts: to seek a momentary victory at the risk of losing the relationship. But Abram was very wise. He recognized that when tensions threaten relationships, bitter quarreling is not likely to be productive in the long run. He felt certain there had to be a better alternative.

4. Give up the lesser to gain the greater. Abram saw another way out. It didn't have to be a question of who's right or who's wrong, who wins or who loses. Within the conflict he recognized a valid concern: because of the sheer numbers of their combined flocks and herds, something had to give. Their previous assumption (that they could move about together) wasn't working. He looked beyond the immediate situation and saw an alternative that met the needs of all concerned. And just like a parent who suggests that one child cut the cake and the other child have first choice, he let the air out of the fear that the choice wouldn't be fair.

"Is not the whole land before us?" (See, the cake is big enough for two pieces.) "Let's part company." (I'll cut the cake.) "If you go to the left, I'll go to the right; if you go to the right, I'll go to the left." (You can have first choice.) Abram let the matter be settled on Lot's terms, in the interests of domestic peace. Yet the matter was settled in a way which was mutually agreeable.

Conflict which is settled by simply giving in to the other or winning the fight at the expense of the other does not lead to peace. Peace is achieved when both parties feel their needs are being met. In Abraham's case, he thought there was plenty of good land to meet his needs. So even if Lot chose the better land, what remained would more than satisfy his goals. He chose to give up something of lesser (getting very good land instead of the very best land) to gain something greater (peace with his relative).

The role of peacemaking is not an easy one to choose, however, for it violates a natural instinct to put up a fight, to make sure we won't be cheated. When we find ourselves in a conflict, our first reaction is often, "Somebody's going to take advantage of me." And so we choose to battle it out as though that were the only path open to us.

But in a world where conflict is epidemic and where family disputes quickly get out of hand, we are called by our Lord to demonstrate that civil war is not always inevitable, and that there is an alternative—the way of peace.

The fact that Lot immediately took advantage both of the offer and of the generosity which prompted it is for the moment beside the point. The significant thing is that Abram took the initiative, and made the offer.

5. Be willing to pay the price. Even though Abram suggested an alternative which would meet the needs of both parties, it was still a costly decision for him. It can be argued, of course, that since

Abram was a wealthy man, he was well able to afford whatever he sacrificed by allowing his nephew first choice of the land. But there was no legal or moral pressure on him to make the offer. After all, Lot too was rich, and he had no more claim to the land than Abram had. It is a rare person who gives up valuable property willingly. No one could have blamed the patriarch if he had stood on his rights, let Lot propose a solution if he could and above all protected that which he had come to think of as his own.

But Abram didn't reason that way. However valuable the property, its worth was not to be compared to keeping peace between them. To him, peace was worth the price, and he paid it. Someone always has to be willing to risk something if family dissensions are to end in restored relationships instead of in bloodletting.

This is true in church quarrels too. In recent years we have often seen the gospel discredited by warring factions within the church who have insisted on taking their disputes to the civil courts in complete contravention of the biblical teaching in 1 Corinthians 6:1-6 ("If any of you has a dispute with another, dare he take it before the ungodly for judgment instead of before the saints?"). These Christians apparently prefer to bring the church's witness into disrepute rather than yielding, for example, on the issue of ownership of church property.

It happens this way: a local congregation decides that it can no longer in good conscience continue as a member of a particular denomination. Immediately there is conflict over whether the church property belongs to the local group or to the larger body. Sometimes the law is clear on the issue, sometimes not. Neither party seems willing to make any concession, and so the case goes to the courts where it drags out for years while newspapers fill their columns with accounts of the bitterness involved. And Satan laughs!

Fortunately, there are exceptions. I witnessed a large center-city church, long noted for its evangelical witness, which took a different route. When that congregation felt led to leave their denomination, they entered into friendly negotiations with the presbytery (representing the denomination), as to a fair disposition of the church property—in this case a very valuable piece of real estate. The congregation and the presbytery opted for a settlement by mutual agreement rather than the scandal of a lawsuit in which each side would have tried to prove its legal rights to the court.

In a settlement among themselves, one side or the other was bound to lose something they might have gained by litigation. But the disagreeing parties chose to pay the price of peace because, to them, that was a small sacrifice compared to a bitter struggle and broken relationships.

Our Savior offers the supreme example here. He brought an end to the awful separation between sinful humanity and a righteous God by paying the price of the settlement himself. He bought peace by giving up that which was rightfully his (Phil 2:6-8), and by putting to his own account the debt we owed (1 Pet 2:24).

6. Take the risk. To take a step toward peace, as Abram did, is always a risky business. Lot might have been suspicious that his uncle's generosity was some sort of scheme to better his own situation. ("What's Abram's real motive in making the offer?") Many of us skeptically examine a generous offer by asking, "What are the strings attached to it? What's the gimmick? Why the sudden generosity?"

There was also the risk that Lot might rebuff his uncle's suggestion, choosing to nourish a grievance (real or imagined) rather than graciously accept the alternative offered by his uncle. Lot might have thought the offer not generous enough! He could have said he needed all the land to adequately graze his herds.

The patriarch had no guarantee that his gesture of kindness would be gratefully received or that the conflict would be averted by it. Lewis Smedes puts it well in his book, *Love within Limits:* "It takes power to be kind, *because* love is risky. Unlike God, we often fail to be kind because we dare not risk the consequences. The driving power of love may move us toward kindness, but stop us short when we consider what might happen to us. . . . The risks in kindness are terrifying."

But this is the only way chasms are crossed and breaches healed. Abram's story illustrates this truth, but the ultimate demonstration is the loving-kindness which God shows toward us. Who can measure the suffering of the triune God, not only at Calvary, but all through the ages, as men and women respond callously to his persistent efforts to reconcile us to himself?

I've seen people take such risks, sometimes with glorious results, sometimes with no apparent reward for their efforts. Jean and Marcia are two such persons.

Jean was already separated from her husband when I first met her. Jack's unfaithfulness to her was beyond dispute. He admitted that while professing fidelity to his wife he had fathered a child by another woman. Moreover, he showed no signs of repentance. It was in such a high-risk situation that Jean offered forgiveness and sought reconciliation with her husband. It was anything but easy to do. She faced the prospect that her already bruised and battered spirit might take another almost unbearable beating if her husband refused her offer. The risk was great. We all rejoiced, then, when Jack was moved by her willingness to forgive him and agreed to make the effort to restore their marriage.

Marcia, on the other hand, offered again and again to pay the price of her husband's moral misdeeds by extending full forgiveness and reconciliation only to have him take advantage of her offer by claiming all the benefits of the marriage relationship while continuing to flaunt its responsibilities.

Yet the fact that Jean's story has a happy ending and Marcia's does not is, in a sense, incidental. For these two women, like Abram and like our Lord on the cross, did the right thing in taking the risk of love, whether or not the response would restore peace. To do what Christ did, in taking on himself the penalty of our sins, does not insure peace between sinful humans and a holy God, for there are always those who reject his proffered love. But to make the offer, regardless of the response, is a godlike thing. There are many varieties of love in the world, but Christ's love is unconditional—and that's always costly and risky.

7. *You won't lose by being generous.* Abram's action and its consequences reminds us of another lesson which Scripture clearly teaches: God is always generous with those who hold their possessions lightly, readily sharing what they have with others, even when they're under no legal obligation to do so. And in the long run, neither Abram nor those who follow his example are any poorer for their generosity. As someone has said, "God will be debtor to no one!"

Paul told the Philippians: "But my God shall supply all your need according to his riches in glory by Christ Jesus" (Phil 4:19 KJV). Some Christians claim that verse as a sort of blank check, an ironclad guarantee that God will make abundant provision for all our needs. But we need to remember that no Scripture is to be understood or applied apart from its context, as though it stood in splendid isolation from all the rest of biblical teaching.

This particular verse is, to be sure, a declaration of God's faithfulness. But it was given to people who had poured themselves out in great generosity to meet the material needs of their beloved friend and missionary, Paul. God's promise to provide for all our needs is intended for those who have refused to hang on selfishly to what God has already given them. This verse offers no get-rich-quick scheme, no promise of material prosperity for all believers. But it is a trustworthy assurance that if you'll let go of what you have to meet the needs of others, God will surely take care of your needs—to a degree that will enable you to continue to be generous.

Abram became a powerful witness to this truth. In the year that followed his generous dealings with Lot, he was richly blessed, materially as well as spiritually. God saw to it that his servant did not lack the resources to be generous to others, even as he had been with his nephew.

There are times when resolving conflict demands a spirit of generosity. I know Christians who pay the price of peace at their own expense and testify joyfully to God's faithfulness. They are not always people with the largest bank accounts. Rather, they are people who marvel at the generosity of God, share what he gives them (often with the undeserving and the unappreciative), and then experience afresh the Lord's generosity! Isn't this exactly what God is saying to us in 2 Corinthians 9:11: "You will be made rich in every way so that you can be generous on every occasion, and through us your generosity will result in thanksgiving to God"?

8. *Persevere in love.* We don't know whether Lot was truly grateful for the way Abram dealt with him. His later history is a sorry one, but the love which moved Abram to make family unity a priority in Genesis 13 was a love which followed Lot even in his darkest hour. In Genesis 19, Lot and his family were imperiled by the wickedness of the environment he had chosen for them. Lot decided to live in Sodom and Gomorrah which turned out to be so wicked that God chose to destroy them. Abram might well have felt justified in leaving his nephew to suffer the consequences of his own bad decisions.

But "love suffers long, and is kind" (1 Cor 13:4 KJV). So Abram, who had been generous with his property, was also generous in his spirit and in his prayers. Instead of leaving Lot to his deserved fate, he cried out to God for his deliverance and that of the pagan cities of Sodom and Gomorrah.

This is unconditional love, love that forgives not seven times but seventy times seven. It takes just such love to maintain and preserve strong family ties. Abram's love is a foreshadowing of the boundless grace of Christ: to Lot it could have been said, "You know the grace of your uncle, Abram," just as the Spirit says to us, "You know the grace of our Lord Jesus Christ" (2 Cor 8:9). This is the kind of persevering grace that it takes to reconcile families and churches, so that peace may dwell where conflict formerly raged.

Abram never had any reason to regret the way he had dealt with Lot. His sensitivity to trouble in the making was rewarded, and his dealing kindly with the undeserving was not in vain. He exemplified a principle which long guided a dear friend of mine: "Never resist a generous impulse!" The one who spoke those words lived that way herself, and taught her family the beauty of such a life.

Remember . . .

There is no cheap, easy solution to our rifts between relatives. But it is infinitely more costly to allow envy to go unchecked, bitter feelings to be aggravated, harsh words to be spoken and never recalled, and our homes and churches to be wrecked by the resultant conflict. The consequences of our unwillingness to go the second mile in reconciliation are much more costly than the price of peace.

Family quarrels, whether in our homes or in our churches, are not often settled by the laws of logic or even by a strict application of justice, but rather by one of the parties in the conflict *taking the initiative* to manifest something of the grace and unconditional love which God shows in his dealings with us. Let's learn from Abram and a host of others that God blesses our willingness to take the first step toward healing the rifts that come between us and those dearest to us.

3

Jumping
the Gun
on Judgments

I PICKED UP THE RINGING PHONE and immediately recognized Lou's voice.

"I've had it, Dr. Fenton!" he said, his voice shaking with rage on the other end. "This is the last straw."

Immediately Lou had my full attention. He had been making valiant efforts to preserve his shaky marriage. But at this moment he seemed ready to concede that the marriage was impossible. I asked what had happened.

"Ginny left the house three and a half hours ago, 'to pick up a few things at the grocery store,' she said—and she's still not back. She knows I'm on emergency call at work, and here I am, stuck home with the kids. If my boss called me on the pager right now, I couldn't leave! And a life might be at stake!"

Could she have had an accident, I wondered, but Lou quickly dismissed the possibility. "Nah, she was upset at me for something or other I did, and left in a huff. She's staying away just to make me pay—but let me tell you, it's going to backfire in her face. I'm not putting up with it!" He said he was so angry that if Ginny walked in at that moment, he would be tempted to blast her—and he didn't specify what form the "blasting" might take!

"What makes me so mad, Dr. Fenton," he said, still fuming, "is that she's probably in a bar someplace, drinking it up with some of her girlfriends, knowing I'm home in a pickle." But when I pressed for any basis he might have for suspecting this, he admitted that he had none. Ginny had been a drinker many years ago, but there had been no recent evidence of such behavior.

"You know, Lou," I suggested, "maybe she's at a friend's home, trying to get over the hurt she's feeling by talking things over with someone she trusts. That seems at least as good as your theory that she's partying it up in some bar."

Gradually he calmed down, and confessed that he had no right to give up hope, at least until he knew with more certainty what Ginny had been doing during those hours. He even admitted (finally) that some of the blame for his wife's grievance was rightly his!

While I haven't inquired specifically into the details of what happened when Ginny got home, I have good reason to believe that Lou, beginning to see things in a more reasonable light, restrained himself from any rash words or actions. He saw that he needed both to deal with his own shortcomings and to listen to her side of the story. In the months since then, it has become apparent that they found a peaceful resolution of the crisis.

The Problem of Quick Judgments
Who knows how much soul-damage has been done through the

centuries by Christians who have passed hasty judgment on the attitudes, actions and motivations of fellow believers! How many families have been destroyed because one member judged another before all the facts were in? How many long-standing friendships have been weakened or even dissolved when the ugly seeds of suspicion were allowed to take root? How many local churches and even denominations have hurt their witness to the world for the same reason?

Such questions are rhetorical, to be sure. But anyone who knows the Christian scene firsthand has too often witnessed the pain caused by those who prematurely rush to judge. If we have any sensitivity at all, we must be aware of our ability to inflict severe wounds in this way.

That was the case earlier in this century, during the Fundamentalist/Modernist controversies. Even though I arrived late on the scene, I still realized that important issues were at stake and that it was essential to speak strongly about the inspiration and authority of the Scriptures, and the deity of Jesus Christ. I have no regrets about having done this. What I *have* had to repent of, along with many other well-meaning defenders of the faith, was my tendency to use guilt-by-association to condemn all those on the "other side." I believed that if a movement was characterized by false teaching, then everyone connected with it must be at fault. At our worst, we used a very broad brush in painting those we disagreed with as heretics. Some of them were, but many were not.

We treated the labels we pinned on others as divinely inspired. We were suspicious of fellow Christians without making any effort to get to know them or listen to their side before condemning them. Sometimes we were too ready to accept charges at face value which were based on the flimsiest of evidence. And we did all this in the name of defending the truth of God!

I hope I shall never be ashamed of taking a stand for the Word of God. My convictions about its trustworthiness, properly interpreted, have grown stronger with the passing years, and I feel no need to apologize for my stand. But I have also learned the need to speak the truth in love.

An Ancient "Church Split"

Israel faced the danger of hasty judgments right after its successful conquest of the Promised Land. Numbers 32 tells us that before the twelve tribes of Israel crossed the Jordan River into Canaan, a minority group composed of the tribes of Reuben, Gad and the half-tribe of Manasseh had asked Moses to be allowed to colonize the land on the east side of the Jordan. The other tribes would possess the land to the west of the river. Moses had agreed to their request on one condition. The smaller group would first join with the others in the conquest of the whole land before settling down on the east side. They accepted.

Once the whole land was subdued, they headed back to the river. On the way home they built an imposing altar on the *west* side of the river bank, "near the Jordon on the Israelite side" (Josh 22:11) before they crossed over to their own land.

News of the altar-building reached the other tribes as they were settling in their newly conquered territory. They immediately interpreted the action as a clear-cut act of rebellion against the Lord. Were they going to worship there instead of at the tabernacle? What was this after all, a rival altar? That would be intolerable. God would be offended.

Feeling ran high, and it was soon decided that all-out warfare against the altar-builders was the only response to the incipient rebellion. So "the whole assembly of Israel gathered at Shiloh to go to war against them" (Josh 22:12).

Somehow, wiser counsel prevailed in Israel. Before taking such

a drastic step, they decided to investigate the situation more carefully. So they confronted the people of Reuben, Gad and Manasseh,
not with spears and swords, but with a strongly worded protest
over their altar-building.

The three tribes emphatically assured their cousins that they did
not build the altar in rebellion to the Lord. " 'On the contrary, it is
to be a witness between us and you and the generations that follow,
that we will worship the LORD at his sanctuary with our burnt
offerings, sacrifices and fellowship offerings' " (Josh 22:27).

Actually, they admitted, they were afraid that at some future
point, the tribes in Canaan (or their descendants) would disinherit
them and forbid them to worship the Lord at the tabernacle, using
the Jordan as an artificial dividing line between those who were
"God's people" and those who were not. They built the altar so that
if that ever happened, they could say, "Look at the replica of the
LORD's altar, which our fathers built, not for burnt offerings and
sacrifices, but as a witness between us and you" (v. 28).

Apparently both the content of their response and the sincerity
with which it was expressed thoroughly satisfied the visiting delegation. Their anger, which had been so close to a flash point,
subsided. They were now convinced that the motivation of the
builders was well-intentioned and represented no threat to the
religious unity of Israel. They were flexible enough to admit that
there were no grounds for their previous charges. Moreover, they
carried a message of full reassurance back to their people.

Note the glorious result of all this: "They talked no more about
going to war against them to devastate the country where the
Reubenites and the Gadites lived" (v. 33). To such a conclusion
only one response seems fitting: "Hallelujah!"

Use Caution in Making Judgments

Conflicts among Christians today don't normally end in bloodshed.

But there is still much to learn from this story of a war that was averted.

1. Learn the difference between "judging" and "discerning." When Jesus said, "Do not judge, or you too will be judged" (Mt 7:1), I don't believe he meant that we are never to make value judgments. By making such judgments we grow in the faith. Our Savior said that a tree is to be judged by its fruit (Mt 12:33), and he warned us not to cast our pearls before swine (Mt 7:6). Obviously, he expects his disciples to know who are and who aren't "swine" and to know the quality of "fruitfulness" in the lives of those who claim to be Christ's followers.

But he *is* warning us against passing judgment on people and groups in a self-righteous way, especially when our knowledge is limited. When we fall into this trap, we make the same mistake as many unbelievers do. In talking with students on secular campuses, I have discovered that many have rejected Christ, not because they have tested the evidence concerning him and found it unconvincing, but solely because they have accepted as fact the untested opinions of other unbelievers.

In the Old Testament story from Joshua, the dispute was not about if the three tribes had built an altar. Rather the offended tribes assumed the motive was wrong for building it and were ready to take action based on their (faulty) judgment. They judged rather than discerned. For Christians to make charges against one another without having a solid basis for doing so, or in a spirit of judgment rather than a desire for reconciliation, is also a grievous mistake. Our guilt as Christians when we make such judgments may be even greater than the sin of those who judge Christ and his witnesses superficially.

We need to develop an awareness of our tendency to make quick judgments and grow in our ability to discern the true nature of a situation. But how? The following steps may be helpful.

2. Beware of mass hysteria. In this and other Old Testament narratives, the people of God proved to be as susceptible to mob psychology and mass violence as any other group throughout history has been. Having received a report that not only displeased them but threatened their faith, they were tempted to react with inordinate haste. On the basis of minimal information, they were ready to strike out at people who had just been their comrades-in-arms, helping them to conquer the land. The measure of God-given unity which had made them a relatively cohesive unit, even amidst the testings in the wilderness, was on the verge of being shattered.

In our day of mass communication through magazines, television, even newspapers, it is easy for a widespread group of Christians to "get the facts" about what a big-name Christian personality said or what this church or that denomination is doing. But this same mass communication makes it difficult for the thousands of readers or viewers to really check out the facts before passing judgment. And sadly, even Christians seem all too ready to denounce a fellow believer or sister group on the first hearsay they encounter.

Obviously we can't close our eyes to "media stories" that affect the Christian community at large, such as the Jim Bakker affair to which even—maybe especially—the secular news agencies gave such wide coverage. But we must be willing to develop a healthy suspension of judgment when our information relies solely on the mass media.

And how many times are controversies sparked among whole congregations by the gossip of one member or the judgment of a few? The apostle James warned, "Consider what a great forest is set on fire by a small spark. The tongue also is a fire . . ." (Jas 3:5-6). We need to be constantly aware that mass opinion can easily be based on minimal information, and alert to the dangers of mass action based on hasty judgments.

3. Speak up for caution. We're not told who should have the credit for issuing a timely word of caution to the Israelites who were arming themselves, urging further investigation before more drastic measures were taken. But somebody spoke up and argued that it was too soon to decide that open warfare was the only possible solution to the problem. Whoever that wise person was, we need thousands like him or her today—in government, in domestic life and in our relationships in the church.

As I read the history of the United States, I can't help wondering whether on a number of occasions the course of international relations might not have been changed for the better if we had heeded the counsel of caution. The whole issue of our participation in the Vietnam War, for instance, is amazingly complex and heavily charged with emotion. To this day there is no overwhelming consensus among statesmen what our course of action should have been. But what if some of our leaders had persuasively argued for a more thorough investigation of the tragic situation and a more careful assessment of the reasons, pro and con, regarding our involvement in it?

Suppose caution had been urged after the incident in the Gulf of Tonkin—an incident which later became quite controversial as to the actual facts—before we committed ourselves to military action by means of President Johnson's Gulf of Tonkin Resolution. Might the subsequent course of events have been different?

Only God knows the answer to such hypothetical questions. But contemplating the thousands and thousands of names inscribed on the Vietnam Memorial in Washington, D.C., might at least persuade us of the need to investigate carefully every other possible alternative before allowing ourselves once again to be swept into bloody conflict. This is not to argue for peace-at-any-price in international relations. It is only to remind ourselves that Israel had reason to rejoice that someone encouraged them to investigate the situation thoroughly before plunging the nation into an unnecessary civil war.

4. Investigate the charges. When my friend Lou called me, sure that his wife was out drinking with her friends and couldn't care less that he was stuck with the kids even though he was on emergency call from work, he was ready to go to war—in this case, the divorce court. But the facts weren't in! I spoke up for caution and urged him to investigate the charges he was making. Even before Ginny came home, he admitted that he had no real basis for coming to that conclusion, and that there were extenuating factors for which he bore responsibility.

The tribes of Israel no doubt felt that it was important to crush the supposed rebellion of the altar-builders in its infancy, and maybe many argued for swift action. But they took time to lay out their charges before the accused, and discovered that they had supposed wrong. Few conflicts in our homes and churches demand such immediate action that taking time to investigate the full situation from all sides isn't the better side of wisdom.

What did Israel do? They sent a delegation to confront the "rebel" tribes face to face. They even made an accusation, and assumed that they were guilty. But nonetheless they still asked the question, "Why? How could you do this?"

Normally, I would encourage a wounded spouse or an angry congregation to ask for the facts *before* jumping to conclusions and making an accusation. But it speaks to me that Israel, even though they were *sure* that the altar was an act of rebellion, still gave their cousins a chance to give an answer for their actions.

Jesus addressed the problem of interpersonal conflict, both when "your brother has something against you" (Mt 5:23) and when "your brother sins against you" (Mt 18:15). In both cases, Jesus said in effect, "Go to the brother or sister in question and talk about it!" In actual practice, when wounded parties go directly to the source and talk to each other about the conflict, new information is often discovered which puts water on the fires of hasty judgments.

5. Practice restraint, not rash actions. In Matthew 18:15-17, Jesus outlined a list of steps to follow if someone sins against us. Three of the steps involve talking together—first just between the parties involved, then with one or two others, then with the whole church—*before* action is taken. And the whole point is not to accuse or condemn, but to reconcile.

In my own relationships with other Christians, I often need the example of the majority tribes in ancient Israel who decided not to go to war with their own people until every other option had been given a chance to work—and I have reason to believe that other believers need it, too!

6. Try a "soft answer." But some of the credit for the peaceful solution of the problem belongs to the minority party as well. When they faced the bitter accusations of the people from across the river (Josh 22:15-20), they didn't respond in anger. (How many of us would be as calm if we were falsely accused?) Instead, they patiently explained their purpose in building the altar (vv. 21-29). They protested their innocence, to be sure, but they did so without heat, and even expressed their willingness to be punished by God himself if, for all their good intentions, they had acted unwisely in building the altar.

When I was a child in Sunday school, I memorized the verse, "A soft answer turneth away wrath" (Prov 15:1 KJV), and I have proved the truth of that word many times in subsequent years. During college, I found summer employment with Curtis Publishing Company, publisher of *The Saturday Evening Post.* My job was to take a crew of slum area youngsters to various neighborhoods in Philadelphia, selling magazines. They weren't the most disciplined adolescents in the world, and occasionally I found myself confronted by irate housewives, bitterly complaining that these dead-end kids had raided their gardens, trampled their grass or muddied their porches.

I learned after a time that the best course of action was to listen sympathetically to their complaints, to be slow to argue with them and not to give in to the temptation to answer their accusations with the same degree of heat they had vented on the boys and me—all this without leaving my boys defenseless, with no advocate to plead their side of the case.

As I saw overheated tempers cool, I learned that nothing is ever gained by answering an accuser with the same intemperate spirit he or she may be showing toward me. I found that there is a way to deal with complaints and criticisms which helps defuse the situation, rather than exacerbating it. I proved, to my own satisfaction, that angry charges are indeed best dealt with by a "soft answer."

7. *Celebrate peace!* There must have been a profound sense of relief on both sides when Phinehas the priest and the rest of the delegation returned to Canaan with the good news that war had been averted. The people who heard this welcome report, to their great credit, gave praise to God for a victory in which neither side had to taste the bitterness of defeat (Josh 22:33). The narrative itself says nothing about the direct intervention of God in the situation, but the people knew that there was no other adequate explanation for the fact that both sides could put away their swords and go back to building their houses and sowing their fields.

The overwhelming truth of the Old Testament, as well as the New, is that the Lord of righteousness is a God of peace who desires for all people the blessing of living out their lives in harmony with one another. The twelve tribes knew this, and when they were able to draw back from the brink of warfare with those of their own nation, their sighs of relief were accompanied by songs of praise. And that was a truly fitting acknowledgement that a greater wisdom than any of them possessed had been at work to bring the matter to such a happy conclusion.

Whenever any of us works for peace among brothers and sisters in Christ, we can be assured that God is pleased with our efforts, even when they are rebuffed. And whenever we seek to bring peace where conflict threatens, we can also be assured that God will not withhold his help from us. Then, when success does crown our efforts, we shall know that all the praise belongs to him.

Remember . . .

We Christians are not called to be peace-at-any-price people. There may indeed be times when conflict with fellow Christians is unavoidable, when we must speak out against sinful actions and attitudes. But many conflicts could be avoided if we would *use caution in making judgments.* Hope for resolving potential conflicts will best be served by taking the steps necessary to truly discern a situation, such as taking time to investigate the charges and avoiding rash actions before all the facts are in. And if we are the ones who are rashly accused, a "soft answer" and being willing to explain our side of the situation may make all the difference between conflict and peace.

When we are tempted to jump to conclusions over the supposed wrongdoing of an individual or group within the church, let's learn from these Old Testament believers, who found a better way.

4

Growing Pains

DISSENSION AMONG CHRISTIANS, whether in the home or in the local church, is almost always a sign that Satan is at work. But apart from his diligent efforts to subvert our unity, there are also "natural causes" which often hinder us from fully enjoying the oneness in Christ we've been promised.

Sometimes the normal processes of growth, in an individual or in a group, introduce elements which create conflict or challenge unity. It isn't only adolescents who suffer growing pains. Churches experience them too, and sometimes the suffering seems almost too great a price to pay for further progress.

I was thrilled to be asked to participate in the first anniversary of a church that was evidently enjoying great blessing from God. Christ Community Church had been founded by a group of committed Christians from Faith Chapel, a strong city church. Their vision was to begin a new work in the affluent and burgeoning suburb of Brookside, where there was no strong corporate witness for Christ. Their challenge was to create a community of God's people in an area characterized by individualism, materialism and self-indulgence.

Starting up hadn't been easy since it meant the relocation of several families, but the group was enthusiastic and hard working. They began small home Bible studies and sharing groups as a way to attract, integrate and disciple new people. The newborn church grew rapidly, many lives were transformed and within a year's time it was apparent that a strong spiritual impact was being made on the community. At the anniversary we celebrated the Lord's goodness for the roots that had been planted and the fruit that was blossoming.

Apparently, leadership resources were overtaxed. So were the facilities available for their meetings. Makeshift arrangements were increasingly unsatisfactory. It was difficult, if not impossible, to provide an adequate program for the various age levels at a time when the community was running over with young parents who were feeling an increasing responsibility to provide for the spiritual needs of their fast-growing families. Everyone yearned for a church property they could think of as "their own." But every improvement which was contemplated—adding to the staff, providing more adequate facilities (whether rented or purchased) or expanding the outreach of the work—demanded increased financial support which didn't always keep up with the projected programs.

These and a number of other difficulties loomed menacingly before the neophyte group. In some areas, solutions were found. In others, well-meaning people found themselves differing as to how to handle the situations, and after a time their differences were exaggerated. Molehills were transformed into mountains as opinions became convictions, and convictions were made dogmas. Suddenly believers were going their separate ways, hardly mourning their loss of unity, and the consequent lack of spiritual impact.

What happened? I'm too far removed from the scene of action to give an absolute answer. But I'm sure that one element was simply the growing pains that are normal for a burgeoning organization. The group found itself faced with a number of vexing problems they hadn't confronted before. They ran out of room for further growth, and seemed to have nowhere to go; they were shorthanded in the area of experienced leadership, and the problem of finding and financing a larger staff seemed overwhelming. The programs that had served them well in the beginning now seemed utterly inadequate for the needs of the new Christians in their family.

It's an old story—at least as old as the situation which threatened to destroy the young church in Jerusalem. They had growing pains too, and that is not to trivialize the problems. For if the consequences of growth aren't effectively handled, the resulting conflict may be very serious.

Growth and Conflict

Luke paints the background in Acts 1—5. The apostles had been boldly declaring the resurrection of Jesus Christ, performing miracles of healing and calling people to repentance. In spite of jailings and persecution, many people believed. And these believers experienced great unity and fellowship. They met daily for prayer and ate together in their homes. They even sold their possessions in order to give to the poor and shared all they had with one another so that no one would be in need. Seeing this love in action, more and more believed and became part of the swelling church.

Then tension developed. In spite of good intentions, some people's needs weren't met. "The Grecian Jews among them complained against the Hebraic Jews because their widows were being overlooked in the daily distribution of food" (Acts 6:1).

Behind this story, many see evidence of Satan's strategy to quench the new movement, before its fire could cover the earth. The evil one certainly likes to take advantage of conflict between Christians. But we do the early church a disservice, and ourselves as well, if we lay the whole business at the devil's doorstep. For the danger that threatened these believers grew out of the blessing of God on their witness, as they grew in numbers and influence day by day. Suddenly there were growing pains—"happy" problems if handled right, "deadly" ones if not solved in God's way.

No Gain without Pain

You see, the early church was already understaffed! Their remarkable growth had quickly outstripped their resources. It wasn't that they didn't have enough preachers. But other aspects of the ministry were being neglected, and a cry of pain went up from one segment of the congregation.

Thus the initial issue—the inevitable staff shortage caused by rapid growth—was an innocent sort of thing, a kind of growing pain. But less innocent elements were also at work, and in them lay the possibilities of a destructive explosion that would tear the young Christian community apart.

The charge was that needy people in the congregation were being neglected. If that charge could be proven, it would signal a potentially volatile situation. For neglect of the helpless quickly becomes a highly charged issue—which is why politicians love to charge their opponents with this. Then too if it could be demonstrated that a group which preached the love of God didn't manifest that love to the needy in its own membership, its witness to the unbelieving world would quickly be discredited.

But there was another explosive factor here. The gospel of Christ had drawn together into fellowship people of diverse linguistic backgrounds, as both Greek-speaking Jews and those who spoke Aramaic found themselves members of the same body. That fact in itself brought a challenge to the unity of the organization, for ever since the Tower of Babel diversity of languages has tended to be a divisive force. Around such differences strong ethnic loyalties and suspicions tend to spring up.

Something of this sort may have been developing in the First Church of Jerusalem, and it now appeared that the glue of the gospel, which had united these believers into one harmonious body, was about to become unstuck.

Hunger and deprivation are always emotionally charged issues. A sense of being discriminated against understandably provokes deep resentment, and doubly so when people feel that they are being treated unfairly because of their race, language or ethnic origins. And so a fairly natural circumstance of rapid growth in the church at Jerusalem threatened to become a major conflict, endangering the very existence of the group.

We ought to note right here that this sort of danger is much more likely to manifest itself in a live, active church than in a moribund group. It is often the church which has been richly blessed by the Lord, its work characterized by great fruitfulness, that finds itself threatened by disunity and division along the way.

A crisis was at hand in the early church. And it all began as growing pains!

We all have growing pains. Growing families develop bathroom scheduling problems that never confronted them before the kids became teen-agers. Growing churches struggle with decision-making in areas where they have little previous experience, and contrary opinions drive wedges of dissension that didn't exist when the group was small.

The significant thing in the story in Acts 6, however, is not the causes of the conflict, but how the early church handled the situation. How did they respond to the complaint? What was the result? What can we learn from our first-century brothers and sisters in Christ?

Dividing the Work

When there is too much to do, you can either stop doing so much or you can get others to help. Sometimes God may be calling us to stop doing so much, to cut back on certain ministries or cancel them altogether. But if it is clear he wants certain kinds of work to continue and grow (as seemed to be the case in Acts), then the solution is to bring others in to help. This sounds deceptively simple. But bringing others in may be costly. It may mean admitting mistakes or giving up some power. But the results may well be worth it. Let's see what happened in first-century Jerusalem.

1. Admit the problem. The apostles weren't perfect or the problem would never have arisen, but they were quick to admit their failure, and they didn't become defensive when the problem was called to their attention. They neither made light of the problem, nor exaggerated its importance. Instead, they took prompt action to deal with it.

2. Recognize the problem as part of normal growth processes. It's a comforting thing to realize that such problems are only to be expected in a growing community, just as certain pains inevitably accompany our bodily growth.

When I entered early adolescence, I was awakened one night by extreme pain in both my legs. I had never experienced anything like it. I was terrified. What if I lost the use of my legs!

When morning came, I related my experience to my parents, who thereupon taught me a few of the basic facts of physiology, and helped me to see that in the growth of my limbs, an inevitable stretching process was taking place in my muscles, tendons and nerves. My pain was a sign not of deterioration and decay but of growth and development. With that kind of reassurance, I could stand the pain!

It's not the dying church that suffers the most severe problems. That group soon loses its ability to feel pain. But a living, growing organism is going to be stretched in a variety of ways and that process may well bring pain with it. That's never a pleasant experience, but the growing church needs to remind itself that this kind of pain may be a sign of progress rather than of weakness.

3. Initiate action. The apostles were sensitive souls, alert to the cries of the neglected and to the potential for conflict and division inherent in the situation. Consequently, they refused to allow delay on their part to destroy the unity of the group.

True leadership insists on dealing with potential trouble at once. It was important at this early stage that the apostles engage in something more productive than hand-wringing. Lamenting a situation is always a poor substitute for dealing with the root of the trouble. Our God is not impressed with cheap words of sympathy, and the needy of the earth are not likely to be, either. Prompt action is called for, and it is the responsibility of wise leadership to initiate it.

A Kentucky mountaineer once testified, "I don't ask the Lord for faith enough to move mountains. I can probably get hold of enough dynamite to do that. But I do ask the Lord for enough faith to move me!" Most of us need to allow the Lord to move us to action, especially if we find ourselves in positions of leadership. Troublesome situations in the church don't usually disappear of their own accord! And while it's essential that we pray about such flash points before we do anything else about them, it's also crucial that as leaders we move promptly under God's guidance to confront the problem, as these apostolic leaders did long ago.

4. Draw on the wisdom of others. The apostles didn't act alone. There was no attempt to announce a settlement of the problem from the heights of Mt. Olympus, as though a solution could be imposed by an elite leadership. Since many were aware of the problem and indeed involved in it, the whole church was enlisted in the search for the solution. "So the Twelve gathered all the disciples together . . ." (Acts 6:2).

Not long ago, controversy among both faculty and students arose over a new addition to the Fuller Seminary curriculum. A class known as MC510, on signs and wonders, dealt with phenomena in what has become known as power evangelism. Taught by John Wimber and Peter Wagner, the course, which included an optional "laboratory" on divine healing, was one of the most popular courses on campus and was endorsed by the faculty members of the School of World Mission. But questions and concerns from the theological faculty continued to surface and came to a head. Deep feelings were involved and committed Christians found themselves in profound disagreement with each other on whether the course should continue.

Decisive action was taken by the president of the seminary. He called all the concerned parties together, and they were invited to grapple publicly with the issue, in a spirit of humility and prayer. As free discussion of the issue was encouraged, new light was thrown on the basic elements of the disagreement. Those who had been openly antagonistic to each other came to understand better the position of their opponents. Out of the discussions the administration finally decided to cancel the course, but created a two-week intensive class on church growth which Wimber and Wagner teach. Because a leader wisely included those involved and drew on the wisdom of others, peace was restored and the situation was actually fruitful.

5. Be clear about priorities. When everyone was assembled, the apostles said, " 'It would not be right for us to neglect the ministry of the word of God in order to wait on tables' " (Acts 6:2). What's this? Were they saying that the church should only be interested in spiritual concerns, not physical needs? Were they saying that distributing food was beneath them as apostles? No, they spoke first to the question of priorities: what was it God wanted *them* to be doing?

There's no way to overstate the fact that the Lord's work is only done effectively when we've each determined what our God-given priorities are. This doesn't mean that all of us are meant to have the same priorities in ministry, except in a general sense. For God has given each of us different gifts, and we serve the Lord most harmoniously when we discover our gifts, allow God to set our priorities, and then give ourselves wholeheartedly to the particular part of the task which he assigns to us.

I once heard David Hubbard, president of Fuller Theological Seminary, say, "In the New Testament the ideal of 'roundedness' or perfection is not found in the individual believer, but in the body of Christ." He pointed out that as individuals, each of us has one or more flat sides. It is the genius of the Holy Spirit in building the church to place us in relation to one another in such a way that our flat sides are compensated for. Together we are rounded into wholeness, the perfection which Christ seeks for his body, the church.

I like that concept and believe it is demonstrated in the wise action which the early church took on this particular occasion. The apostles saw their top priority as teaching and preaching the Word, and they made it plain that they intended to continue concentrating on this part of the task. But in saying this, they weren't for a moment declaring that the feeding of the widows was not of great concern to them and to the church. Nor were they insensitive to unfairness in the distribution system. But they were saying that this ministry was not to be a primary responsibility of the apostolic leaders, even though it was indeed a primary responsibility of the church.

In other words, not everyone in the church is meant to do everything—a principle which many harried Christians in the church today have yet to discover!

The work of those who teach and preach is tremendously important. But then, so is the work of the deacons who serve those with physical and material needs. Indeed, the effectiveness of the ministry of the Word will in some measure depend on the way in which all the needs of the believers, both spiritual and material, are met. The most faithful teaching and preaching may be nullified if the leadership is insensitive to other needs of the congregation, particularly those of minority groups within the congregation.

On the other hand, it is surely not enough to feed the widows and do other good works and neglect the Bread of Life. The apostles and the deacons are meant to be complementary, not competitive, in carrying out of their respective ministries. Preaching the gospel and meeting material needs are never to be seen as making rival demands on the time, energy and funds of the church. The group of believers which treats these two callings as somehow in conflict with each other is sowing the seeds of dissension within its own ranks because it has lost sight of the full-orbed nature of the ministry to which God has called the church.

6. *Delegate responsibilities.* So what did the apostles suggest? "Brothers, choose seven men from among you who are known to be full of the Spirit and wisdom. We will turn this responsibility over to them and will give our attention to prayer and the ministry of the word" (Acts 6:3-4).

Management experts in business preach the importance of delegation, that is, dividing authority and responsibility among those who by their varying gifts and special training are particularly equipped to do a particular aspect of the overall task. The wise executive knows better than to try to carry the whole burden of the enterprise on his or her own shoulders.

But long before the schools of business administration had discovered the importance of delegation, Scripture taught it as a basic principle in the service of God. When Moses tried to carry the burden of judging Israel as though it was solely his responsibility, he was rebuked by his father-in-law, Jethro, who said he was going to wear himself out. Jethro then offered this constructive counsel: assign parts of the tasks to others, and then, having instructed and encouraged them, expect them to share the burden of government (Ex 18:13-26). Centuries later the Jerusalem church applied this basic principle.

Why are some churches in the twentieth century so slow to share authority and responsibility? There is a connection between our failure in this area and the high rate of burnout in Christian work. We must learn that some of the church's business is unfinished because of our failure to delegate, and failure to utilize the varied gifts of our members is a prime cause of dissension that often characterizes our ranks.

It's a deadly thing when a pastor tries to do all the work of the church himself. The inevitable result is that much of the work remains undone, to the great dissatisfaction of segments of the congregation. This is not hypothetical. I have recently watched, in one particular church, the relations between pastor and people steadily deteriorate because of his refusal to share the responsibility for the multiple ministries of that church with gifted members.

There is a flip side to this problem as well. Some church members think the professional clergy *should* be doing all the ministry. (They haven't been visited unless they've been visited by the pastor. If someone is hospitalized, it's the pastor's duty to go see them.) But according to Ephesians 4:11-13, there are various kinds of ministers, and these ministers are "to prepare God's people for works of service, so that the body of Christ may be built up." No one in the body is meant to be idle, and no one is meant to do everything!

7. Set high standards for leaders. When the apostles delegated responsibility, they refused to relax their high standards for the service of the Lord. They insisted that those who were to feed the widows be persons of good reputation, "known to be full of the Spirit and wisdom" (Acts 6:3).

Does this make sense? Did the early church need to be so demanding in the criterion it set for choosing those who would be handing out goods to the needy? Why be so finicky? We can understand that to be able to preach the Word effectively one needs to be filled with the Holy Spirit, but to insist on such high standards for those who are to be servants of widows would seem strange indeed to many present-day church nominating committees.

And that may be part of why the church suffers so many conflicts today! We too easily forget that to serve Christ in any capacity, and to please him in doing so, we need special enabling from him. Those deacons were not going to be just servants of widows. They were also going to be servants of God. God took one of those deacons, Philip, and made him a fruitful evangelist perhaps because Philip first manifested the fruit of the Spirit in the service of needy church members.

God's work must be done in God's power if it is to enjoy his blessing—and if unnecessary future conflicts among the believers are to be avoided. This is not to claim that every kind of Christian service demands the same degree of spiritual maturity. An elder in the church undoubtedly needs certain spiritual capacities which will not be demanded, to the same degree, of an usher. But ushers who are filled with the Spirit, and deacons who know their utter dependence on the Lord, will do their work not only to please God, but in a sensitive and efficient way which keeps destructive criticism of their efforts at a minimum.

And so, "They chose Stephen, a man full of faith and of the Holy Spirit; also Philip, Procorus, Nicanor, Timon, Parmenas, and Nicolas from Antioch, a convert to Judaism" (Acts 6:5).

8. *Dedicate leaders to effective ministry.* As part of grappling with the problem of incipient disunity, the apostles rededicated themselves to the ministry of the Word: "We will turn this responsibility over to [these seven men] and will give our attention to prayer and the ministry of the word" (6:3-4). Then, as the church chose the ones who would serve, "They presented these men to the apostles, who prayed and laid their hands on them" (6:6).

Not only did the apostles delegate responsibility for the widows, but they dedicated this service and those who would serve to God and the assembled body, and at the same time dedicated themselves to the ministry God had given as their priority. The widows would no longer be overlooked, but neither would the ministry of the Word suffer. In doing so they made themselves accountable, not only to God, but to the church for effective ministry.

Spiritual leadership in itself is not a guarantee that a group of believers will not be torn apart, since even good leaders are fallible. All human leadership is flawed by its very humanness and stands under the constant judgment of God. The leaders of any Christian organization must hold themselves open constantly to evaluation and judgment of the larger body. That accountability is supremely to God, but it is also to our brothers and sisters in Christ.

Remember . . .
What was the result of addressing the "growing pain" and its potential for disunity in such a way? "The word of God spread. The

number of disciples in Jerusalem increased rapidly, and a large number of priests became obedient to the faith" (Acts 6:7).

The lessons of Acts 6 are desperately needed by the contemporary church. We are still not sufficiently sensitive to the cries of the marginalized, those who feel that even in the church of Christ they are being overlooked. We still have pastors who are trying to care for all the needs of the church themselves—either killing themselves doing so or guaranteeing that important aspects of the ministry will be overlooked, with the result that many believe they are neglected. And we still have too many church members burning out in their hectic efforts to serve the Lord, because they have never recognized that their service is meant to have limits and be tailored to the specific gifts God has given them.

The work of the Lord demands that the needs of his suffering people be met, lest they perish, and disunity rend the church. *Dividing the work:* addressing the problems, searching for solutions together with the whole body and delegating responsibilities to Spirit-filled members, so that the task may be done effectively and the spiritual, emotional and physical health of the workers—as well as the unity of the church—be safeguarded.

5

When Doctrine Divides (Part 1): The Threat to the Church

IN LATIN AMERICA THEY TELL a story about a peasant farmer whose hobby was raising gamecocks. Each year he entered them in the cockfights during fiesta time in a town some miles from his home. On one particular occasion, don Manuel was especially proud of two birds which he had trained throughout the year, with high hopes that one of them would win top honors in the annual competition.

On the morning of the contest, he trussed up each of his prized fowl, carefully binding their legs so they would survive the trip to town without harm to themselves or each other. He then carefully placed them in the trunk of his battered old car and drove slowly to the scene of the competition in order not to excite his potential champions on the way. He was confident that he would return home that night with a blue ribbon and a cash prize.

When he arrived at the cockpit, the crowds were already gathering for the day's contests. He parked his car near the scene of the action and excitedly opened the trunk, already dreaming of how he would spend his prize money.

He was utterly unprepared for the sight that greeted him. Somehow the cocks had broken free of their bonds and the trunk was a sorry mess of blood, chicken flesh and feathers. It was immediately evident that neither of his prized possessions would survive to participate in the competition that day.

Heartbroken, don Manuel surveyed what the two gamecocks had done to each other. Tears coursed down his weathered cheeks, and the only sound that escaped his mouth was a pathetic exclamation, "It's too bad I didn't tell them they were both on the same team!"

On the Same Team?

I felt somewhat as don Manuel did during my freshman year at college. As a reporter on the college newspaper, I had been given an assignment which I suspect no one else on the staff wanted—covering the annual congregational meeting of the college church. Ordinarily, such a gathering would have had no great interest for the students, but this was to be no ordinary meeting. Dissension over doctrinal issues had brought the congregation to the brink of open warfare.

So I had a ringside seat, not at a gory boxing match, but at a bitter conflict where brothers and sisters in the family of God were arrayed against each other, each side avowing its own orthodoxy while impugning the beliefs and behavior of the other. The combatants were respected Christian leaders from the community, some of them my professors. Soon they were at each other's throats. The atmosphere became charged with hate as accusations and countercharges mounted in number and intensity.

It was a sobering experience for a young Christian like me. I was exposed for the first time to the ferocity which can characterize battles between believers—especially when the realm of doctrine becomes the battlefield. I felt like crying out, "Somebody please tell them they're on the same team!" They needed to be reminded that God called them not to fight with each other but rather to unite their forces against the world, the flesh and the devil.

Undoubtedly, I was naive. After all, doctrine is the backbone of the Christian faith, and people are usually ready to fight for dearly held convictions. Later, in seminary, I learned that Christians down through the centuries had often engaged in violent doctrinal disputes with other Christians. It seems that nothing triggers bitterness among God's people like battles over cherished beliefs!

But there must be a better way of handling our doctrinal differences than by denouncing and despising one another! If history reminds us that such conflicts often arise, Scripture shows us a more Christlike way of dealing with our disagreements.

To be sure, the Bible offers no neat formula, guaranteed to work in every situation. But it does allow us the privilege of seeing the first-century church handle its doctrinal conflicts in ways which neither compromise the truth nor destroy the unity of the believers.

This chapter, and the two following, will consider how the early Christians dealt with a potentially explosive situation where doctrine was the issue, involving a serious threat to the young church.

Sincere Diversity versus Divisive Pluralism

In Acts 15:1-5, we learn that some Judean Christians traveled to Antioch and began teaching the Gentile Christians there, " 'Unless you are circumcised, according to the custom taught by Moses, you cannot be saved' " (v. 1). Now this upset Paul and Barnabas and they got into a hot debate with these men. After all, put yourself in their sandals. You've planted a church in a foreign country, new believers are being baptized and growing in the faith, and there is a spirit of freedom and joy in the gospel. Then along come some Lone Ranger teachers from back home telling the new converts that they have to wear suits and ties and sit in pews, or they can't be saved!

But let's not make light of the issue. For centuries circumcision had been the sign for the Jews of being God's called-out people. Nonetheless, the apostles were convinced that in God's acceptance of the Gentiles as "children of Abraham" by pouring out his Spirit upon them, and in the Gentiles' joyful acceptance of the gospel, physical circumcision was no longer required.

In spite of Paul's clear insistence all through his letters that salvation is by grace through faith plus nothing, we still try to add on something of our own doing—as though what Christ has done is not enough. We say, in essence, "Believe on the Lord Jesus Christ and sign our church's doctrinal statement, and you'll be saved," or, "Believe on Christ and submit to our church's list of taboos and you'll be saved," or ". . . and accept our form of baptism," or ". . . and adopt our view of the Second Coming" or some other addition. Human pride pretends to accept the grace of God, provided it can add a few postscripts to the good news.

But this is not the gospel! In Antioch, it threatened to shackle the believers again with legalism by demanding that they submit to the law in order to win the favor of God. It called them to put part of their confidence in their own self-effort, rather than placing their full trust in Christ as the all-sufficient expiation for their sins.

So it was no minor issue that was disturbing the saints in Antioch. The challenge of such false teaching could not be ignored because there could be no détente between the heresy of salvation by human effort and the good news of reconciliation by God's grace alone.

1. Allow for diversity. Given all that I've written so far in this book, it should not be surprising that I recommend giving others the benefit of the doubt when disagreeing with them. After all, there are areas where Christians may in good conscience differ! The nature and form of baptism, the details of God's prophetic timetable, the extent of our call to nonviolence and the use of spiritual gifts are subjects Christians have disagreed about for centuries. All of these issues have at times created divisions and bitter feelings in the church.

Yet at their best, believers have demonstrated that they *can* hold firm convictions about such matters while still respecting other Christians who espouse contrary views. In such cases, the unity of the body need not suffer. In our heart of hearts, we recognize with Paul that we know only in part, and that "we see through a glass, darkly" (1 Cor 13:12 KJV). The Lord seems to be patient with our disagreements in such areas, and we have learned to live with a certain amount of diversity in the church concerning these things.

We had to learn lessons along this line in Latin America when the use of charismatic gifts threatened to become a divisive issue about twenty-five years ago. Many of the churches to which the Latin America Mission (LAM) was intimately related were being swept by a wave of indigenous Pentecostal enthusiasm marked by amazing numerical growth, many heartwarming conversions and the claim to certain gifts (tongues, healing, exorcism and so on). At times, the manifestation of these gifts seemed to produce miraculous deliverances. On other occasions, the consequences seemed to be unhealthy.

Most of the missionaries with LAM had come from noncharismatic backgrounds and had been taught that these gifts had ceased at the end of the first century. We had been led to believe that the kind of thing we were seeing, especially in the churches in Colombia, ought to be condemned in the strongest terms and rooted out of the church wherever it might appear.

It was a tense situation at times, with some missionaries deeply concerned about what they perceived to be excesses at best and the work of the Enemy at worst. But national believers, convinced that God was working in and through them in new and wonderful ways, were deeply distressed by the apparent lack of support by missionaries whom they loved and respected.

All the evangelical mission boards in Latin America were facing the same phenomenon and were handling it in different ways. The situation threatened to produce great bitterness and conflict within the body of Christ. It was the sort of setting in which Christians often fail to remember that they're on the same team! It seemed altogether possible that a work which God had richly blessed through the years would be brought to ruin.

By the grace of God, the missionaries with LAM and their national brothers and sisters continued to love each other, and both sides were kept from bitter attacks on Christians of differing opinions. Without sinful compromise of personal convictions, Christians learned to have full respect for each other, even when they couldn't agree on particular points of doctrine. A God–given love for other members of his family won out. Christians found themselves enabled by the Lord to recognize a place for diversity, given the limited knowledge of all parties concerned.

I first met Francis Schaeffer, the widely known author and defender of the faith, some years ago in England where we were speakers at a pastors' conference. We fell into conversation after one of the evening meetings, and he frankly told me that he was somewhat concerned about some of the practices of the Latin America Mission, which I was General Director of at that time. In particular, he felt strongly that in our city-wide evangelistic campaigns we had compromised our testimony by welcoming the cooperation of some denominational groups which he found doctrinally suspect.

We discussed the matter long and late, and, by the grace of God, without rancor. After some hours, we acknowledged to each other that we shared, perhaps in equal measure, a passion for both the purity and the unity of the church of Christ. It was evident, however, that we drew the line at different places when it came to the question of where to join with others in the Lord's service, and where, in good conscience, we had to separate from them. On that note, and with mutual respect for each other's position, we parted.

In one sense, it was an unsatisfactory conclusion, since we were no closer to an agreement on the disputed issues than we had been at the beginning. From another standpoint, however, we had a new respect for each other's deeply held convictions, and our right as Christians to hold differing views without bitterness. Perhaps we both learned a valuable lesson that night.

The Latin Christians discovered that by the grace of God they could work together for the evangelization of their country and rejoice in each other's fruitfulness. As we saw in the last chapter, while no individual Christian is completely well rounded, the body of Christ should be. That means diversity is a necessity. As my friends in Latin America discovered this, God worked a spiritual victory for all concerned.

Admittedly, however, such pluralism must have well-defined limits. But let no one pretend that it is always easy to draw the line between that which is negotiable in the realm of religious conviction and that which isn't. If such a task were always a simple one, the number of our disagreements with fellow Christians over doctrinal matters would be drastically reduced. But our difficulty in knowing what is absolutely essential to our faith often constitutes a summons to battle. And the Bible provides us with no simple formula for knowing the difference between those issues which ought to be a trumpet call to arms and others which, however vexing they may be, are meant to teach us patience with one another and tolerance for differing views.

2. Drawing the line. How do we tell when diversity is good or when it has gone beyond acceptability? Paul clearly taught that some convictions are peripheral and should not be allowed to cause conflict in the church. For instance, in the early Roman church sincere Christians strongly differed about whether a Christian dared eat meat that had been offered to idols. Paul insisted that such disagreement should be a call to loving forbearance rather than to pitched battles among believers (Rom 14:1-12). He also urged the Colossians not to be unduly concerned about feasts, fasts, special days and other observances, lest differences on these things tear the delicate fabric of Christian unity (Col 2:16-23). Judgment in these matters was to be left to God.

But there is another side to the story. The events in Acts 15 teach us that distinctions can be made, and therefore must be made in settling certain disputes. When disagreements deal with the nature of Christ, the significance of his death or the authority of his teaching, the clear teaching of Scripture is to be definitive. Such issues might be discussed and debated, but the truth is not determined by popular vote.

In the early church, any teaching which diluted or denied the revelation which the apostles had received from God was to be resisted—to the death if need be. Paul and Barnabas insisted that there was no room in the church at Antioch for two conflicting messages competing for the hearts and minds of the people. This was where the line had to be drawn. Like Martin Luther centuries later, they said: "Here we stand. We can do no other!"

Over fifty years ago, a panel of distinguished laymen chaired by William Hocking, brilliant professor of philosophy at Harvard University, was appointed to make a study of the state of Christian missions throughout the world. Their report, entitled "Rethinking Missions," sent shock waves throughout the Christian world. To those committed to biblical authority, the report seemed a calculated attempt to cut the nerve of the missionary enterprise throughout the world by denying the uniqueness of Jesus Christ and urging some kind of synthesis of the major religions of the world while ignoring or denying the clear teaching of Scriptures.

Christians worldwide banded together to expose the unbiblical nature of the report. They challenged the universalism of its findings, with its blatant denial of the authority and saving work of Jesus Christ. They fought a pluralism which denigrated the gospel by which they knew themselves to be saved. A line was drawn—unbelief, masquerading as Christian faith, must not be tolerated. Those who defended the faith against the claims of the report deserve our heartfelt gratitude. They knew that pluralism has its limits.

But we need great wisdom in our churches and denominations today to discern these limits, for too often *pluralism* is a synonym for doctrinal indifference. Self-proclaimed unbelievers are ordained on occasion to what is still called the gospel ministry, with their heresy excused as just another manifestation of pluralism—often without even a whisper of protest by true believers. In the name of tolerance for divergent viewpoints, unbelievers infiltrate a congregation's membership roll, determine its policies, and too often dilute its message. It is time for someone to cry, "Stop!"

Sensing that delay meant danger, the Christians at Antioch moved promptly to resolve the deep divergence that threatened the life and witness of the group. In doing so, they took a first step toward restoring and then maintaining the health of the church.

3. Acknowledge dependence on the larger church. The Antioch church didn't try to settle the issue by a full-scale debate within the local congregation. Instead, "Paul and Barnabas were appointed, along with some other believers, to go up to Jerusalem to see the apostles and elders about this question" (Acts 15:2). They knew they needed the wisdom of more experienced Christians, and they were humble enough to seek competent counsel from those who had walked with the Lord longer than they had.

This was humility, but it was more. Their action recognized the interdependence of the members of the body of Christ. The Bible is insistent on this—we desperately need each other. But we have been so conditioned to pride ourselves on our independence that we forget how unscriptural such an attitude may be, and how we impoverish ourselves in the Christian pilgrimage by not gladly acknowledging how much we need each other.

Some churches call themselves independent. Most of us know what they mean, of course. They're saying that they're not related to any denomination. But in another sense, there's no such thing as an "independent" church. Christians are people who have signed a Declaration of Dependence—dependence on God and on each other, including those who are outside our immediate circle of fellowship. Our churches, as well as their individual members, need healthy relationships. Such relationships obviously don't have to be organizational, but they do need to be recognized, acknowledged and made practical. This is exactly what the congregation at Antioch did when they called for the help of the saints at Jerusalem.

The body of Christ is not just a fellowship to be enjoyed. It is meant to be a sharing, caring community where guidance is readily available from others who have been over the road before us. We need to know that our brothers and sisters in Christ are on call, and we need to take full advantage of their availability, especially when doctrinal differences threaten our unity. Let's face it: the "guidance" which we often claim as individuals is highly subjective. Too frequently it reflects an attempt to justify our long-held prejudices, or to rationalize attitudes and actions which may be more a product of our own desires than of the leading of God. We need the objective counsel of other believers who are not immediately involved in the situation which embroils us.

In recent years I have been aware of some encouraging attempts on the part of Christians embroiled in controversy to reach out to fellow believers to help them resolve their difficulties. One such incident involved Dr. Anthony Campolo, a Christian college professor who is widely known for his fruitful ministry far beyond the campus. Certain Christian leaders called into question a book he had written. They felt it had doctrinal deficiencies serious enough to bar him from speaking at a national youth congress in the summer of 1985. Some of the critics used the word *heresy* in describing it; others criticized it in milder terms.

Campolo defended his position while at the same time welcoming constructive criticism concerning it and declaring that he was open to correction if he could be shown to have taken any unbiblical positions. Evangelical leaders were drawn into the controversy, some defending Campolo, others joining his critics.

The situation deteriorated, threatening to become a knockdown, drag-out fight. Opinions may still differ as to whether such a tragedy was completely averted. Nevertheless, the debate was tempered by those who were concerned with both the doctrinal issues and the threat of disruption in the body of Christ. A panel of three highly respected Christian leaders was asked to meet with Campolo and with his critics to help all concerned understand the issues, and to minister constructively both to the accused and his accusers.

The key lesson here is that those involved in the controversy reached out for help, recognizing that their fellow believers might bring to the matter an objectivity they lacked. Instead of a heresy trial, characterized by a spiritual blood bath, these Christians turned from debate to a sincere attempt to seek mediation. At the very least, they gave opportunity for a pastoral ministry to be exercised to all concerned, and for this, God be praised!

It's interesting to note that when the Antioch Christians sent a commission to Jerusalem to seek help, they didn't settle for a two-man team. Although Barnabas and Paul may have been clear about the issue, perhaps others in the church were genuinely confused. The purpose of the commission was not to have the parent church rubber stamp a conviction already arrived at by Paul and Barnabas, but to help others in the Antioch congregation to see the issues clearly, and to come to a position that would please God and advance the gospel.

In Jerusalem, the team from Antioch found a warm welcome awaiting them (Acts 15:4). The saints in the mother church made it plain that they were glad to see their fellow believers and that they had both the disposition and the time to help them. Many a present-day church, racked by dissension, could likewise profit from the loving ministry of a neighboring group who would provide concern and a listening ear.

4. Celebrate what God is doing even in the midst of current difficulties. The group from Antioch were evidently not problem-oriented. "As they traveled through Phoenicia and Samaria, they told how the Gentiles were being converted. This news made all the brothers very glad" (v. 3). And when they appeared before the church at Jerusalem, they felt no compulsion to introduce the story of the conflict at Antioch immediately. Instead, "they reported everything God had done through them" (v. 4). In spite of the issue which had brought them there, the Antioch committee gave priority to lifting their hearts and those of their fellow believers in thanksgiving to God. Then, with the doxology still ringing in their ears, they moved into the realm of discussion and debate.

In every age, there are times when the airing of theological controversy is necessary. We need what David Augsburger has called "the courage to confront." But we can learn from this group in the early church who chose to conduct the confrontation in an atmosphere bathed in love and praise, and this made a great difference in the outcome.

I can't help wondering how different the consequences might have been if the meeting of the college church congregation mentioned earlier in this chapter had begun with a time of praise. What if those on both sides of the controversy had been invited to share what they had seen the Lord doing in recent days in their lives and ministries? It's hard for saints to be bitter toward each other when they're praising the Lord together for his work in their midst!

Remember . . .
If the experience of the Antioch Christians has anything to say to us in our present-day controversies, it may well be in the form of a threefold exhortation: discern the difference between sincere diversity and divisive pluralism; seek help not only from the Lord but also from experienced Christians who are not involved in the conflict; and focus our attention first on what the Lord is doing in our midst. We surely honor him if we rejoice in his continued faithfulness, even in the midst of current difficulties.

Remembering these points sets a healthy context for resolving differences. But how do we actually go about settling the dispute itself? In the next chapter we will consider the steps the first-century Christians took to answer the question about how Gentiles enter full fellowship.

6

When Doctrine Divides (Part 2): A Fair Hearing

THE LEADERS' COUNCIL IN A CHICAGO CHURCH had been tied up for years around the issue of men's and women's roles. The leaders simply could not agree among themselves on a theological or practical direction for their church. Among the congregation, the topic was rarely discussed. Everyone knew it was a hot issue and was afraid that if it was brought into open debate, bottled feelings would be unleashed and unity would crumble.

Finally the leaders agreed on one thing: it was wrong not to bring the issue out into the open. They scheduled a series of congregational meetings in which three papers would be presented, representing different biblical viewpoints. Then each of the leaders on the council, both men and women, shared their personal experience and points of view. Finally various persons in the congregation shared their responses. The proceedings and papers from each of the meetings were collected and placed in the church library for public review.

The process was not without pain. People said things that threatened others. The end result did not fully satisfy some, though progress was made to meet needs that had been identified. But everyone expressed a great deal of appreciation for the process. The issue wasn't under wraps anymore. They had a chance to hear from one another. People with different viewpoints said they felt heard.

Unfortunately, many of us are poor listeners, especially to those who disagree with us. Debate, even among Christians, tends to degenerate into a series of alternating monologs with neither side really hearing the other. And especially when we discuss doctrinal issues, our tendency is to show our impatience with our opponents' position by interrupting their presentation in order to introduce our counterarguments.

Ignoring James's instruction to "be quick to listen, slow to speak" (Jas 1:19), we are often quick to speak and slow to listen. Frequently this means we are not as secure in our own position as we would like to be. It is only when we are reasonably certain of the rightness of our own case that we can afford to be generous in allowing others to present theirs.

Give Both Sides a Fair Hearing
In the last chapter we began a discussion of a doctrinal disagreement in the first-century church. Some thought circumcision was needed before one could become a Christian. Paul and others felt this was equivalent to salvation by works. Note the way discussion of vital issues was handled: "Then some of the believers who belonged to the party of the Pharisees stood up and said, 'The Gentiles must be circumcised and required to obey the law of Moses.'

The apostles and elders met to consider this question. After much discussion Peter got up and addressed them . . . The whole assembly became silent as they listened to Barnabas and Paul . . . When they finished, James spoke up . . ." (Acts 15:5).

You get the impression from this account that when the church faced the question of the basis on which Gentile believers would be received into their fellowship, both sides got a fair hearing. A lot of listening as well as a lot of speaking characterized the debate.

Note that the discussion was between opposing groups of *believers*. Verse 5 recognizes the circumcision defenders as part of the Christian family. But it also tells us that they were of the Pharisees' party, and it is evident that they had brought much religious and cultural baggage with them into their new life. They didn't recognize the difference between these beliefs and the essence of the gospel.

It's all too easy to do that! As a missionary in Latin America I had to learn, sometimes painfully, that I had attached some elements of my North American culture to the truth in Christ. There was a time, for instance, when I was completely confounded because the church I was working with had no worship service! You can't have a church without a worship service, I thought. Sunday morning was given over entirely to Sunday school, and Sunday evening there was an evangelistic service. But there was no worship of the kind I was used to—at 11 A.M.! I argued so long for a change that finally the church leaders gave in, and scheduled a twenty-minute worship service on Sunday mornings. Afterward their attitude was, "Okay, we did what you wanted. Are you satisfied?"

It took me a long time to realize that they felt no need for the particular format I called worship. In their homes and in their Bible studies during the week they had plenty of fellowship, prayer and praise. In my inexperience, I was in danger of forcing on my Latin American brothers and sisters elements that were not part of the gospel, but only structures that my North American Christian culture had mistakenly confused with biblical truth.

1. Allow for adequate discussion. Observe the way our first-century brethren conducted the debate. First, those who were attempting to Judaize the Gentiles stated their proposition (v. 5). There followed a lengthy discussion of the issue (vv. 6–7). We are not told what was said or who said it, but the impression is left that those of the Pharisees' party had full opportunity to make their case; *and it was only* after a lengthy discussion that the apostles stated their position.

This procedure is too often a rarity in Christian circles today. Even in church business meetings, steamrollering the opposition is all too common. This is sometimes accomplished by arranging the agenda so that one side gets a full opportunity to state its case and present its arguments while the other side is crowded out by parliamentary maneuvering. I have heard that in the annual meetings of one large denomination, some issues have been postponed until after midnight so discussion may be cut off and certain decisions forced through. Whether such a charge has any basis in fact, I do not know, but mischief is already done if such a suspicion sounds credible.

The first of the apostles to speak was Peter (v. 7). This in itself should be no great surprise. He had already established a reputation for a ready tongue, blurting out the first thing that came to his mind whether it made any sense or not. (Someone has said that we're never so voluble as when we don't know what to say!) It may have been difficult for him to restrain himself while the "much discussion" was going on.

But this is not the Peter of pre-Pentecost days. This is a man now filled with the Spirit, and he has learned that the Spirit restrains, as well as impels, the obedient disciple. Not only are the steps of a good man ordered by the Lord (Ps 37:23), but his "stops" as well!

2. Ask basic questions. When Peter did speak, he raised two basic questions. The first was: *"How has God dealt with this issue in the past?"*

That's not a bad question to raise about any issue which puzzles the church. This doesn't mean that by looking up the index or the concordance in the back of our Bibles we can find an exact parallel to the problem that threatens to divide us. It does mean that just as a lawyer preparing his case seeks for legal precedents to his contemporary situation, so we can often discern the mind of God by discovering what he has revealed by his words and actions in earlier times. If we are serious about this, then all we need do is engage in a fresh, methodical study of the Scriptures, seeking divine precedents which are relevant to the issue now dividing us from our brothers and sisters in Christ.

Peter didn't have to search too far. " 'You know that some time ago,'" he said, " 'God made a choice among you that the Gentiles might hear from my lips the message of the gospel and believe. God, who knows the heart, showed that he accepted them by giving the Holy Spirit to them, just as he did to us. He made no distinction between us and them, for he purified their hearts by faith' " (Acts 15:7-9). The point made by the apostle here was a powerful one. It had all the authority of God's own previous action behind it.

Then Peter in effect asked another basic question: *"What are the consequences likely to be of following the course of action which is being presented here?"* After all, the old proverb, "Look before you leap!" ought to have some application in spiritual matters!

Peter had done his homework, and he had a ready answer to his own implied question. " 'Now then, why do you try to test God by putting on the necks of the disciples a yoke that neither we nor our fathers have been able to bear? No! We believe it is through the grace of our Lord Jesus that we are saved, just as they are' " (vv. 10–11).

Some of his hearers might have wanted to argue the point, but Peter knew that if they were honest with themselves, they would admit that the burden of keeping the law had resulted in frustration, disillusionment and despair. Why ask the Gentiles to carry a load the Jews themselves had been unable to bear?

When troubled about contradictory counsel concerning a course of action in the church, we too should ask, "How has such a proposal worked out in the past? What were its consequences?" It is a foolhardy group which never learns from history!

3. Listen to godly witnesses. Next, Paul and Barnabas spoke up (v. 12). Their words are in a sense another stanza of their previous hymn of praise to the Lord about what he was doing among their Gentile brothers and sisters (vv. 3–4), but now their audience probably saw more clearly the connection between their joyous report and the current controversy. Their stress now was not just on the fact that God had done great things through their ministry, but that he had done these things among the Gentiles—people who were previously cut off from God. And they were eyewitnesses of all this! Their audience listened in rapt silence, knowing that these two men were disciples upon whose ministry the blessing of God had rested in unusual measure.

In controversies today, we often find ourselves confused by the fact that church leaders take widely different positions on the issue at stake. We find ourselves asking, "Whom should I believe? Whom should I follow?"

There's no easy answer to that question, but we may find light by giving special weight to those whose fruitful service for the Lord gives increased authority to their arguments. This is not an infallible test, to be sure, for God often uses strange instruments, and fruitfulness is no guarantee of infallibility on any given issue. But a person's usefulness for God can be a significant element in coming to a decision.

Some years ago, I found myself greatly enriched by the ministry of a particular servant of God. Dr. Charles was not the most eloquent preacher I had ever heard nor was he the most gifted Bible teacher. Sometimes the positions he took varied from those of others more famous. But I found that he had an impact on my life because of the holiness of his life and the fruitfulness of his ministry. He wasn't always right in the positions he took, of course (who is?), but my knowledge of his own pilgrimage gave him great credibility with me.

I suspect it was that way with the audience that Paul and Barnabas addressed. Caught in the crosscurrents of Christian opinion, they would give the reasoning of men like these special weight.

4. Test experience with Scripture. If I had been listing the order of speakers here, and wanted to put the most effective presentation at the end, I don't think I would have chosen James for the wind-up argument. Nothing against James, of course, but I probably would have felt that either Peter or Paul would have been more persuasive in moving the council toward a biblically based position. But the Spirit doesn't always do things the way we would, and it's obvious that God's choice, not mine, was the wise one!

Peter, Paul and Barnabas had largely based their counsel on their own experience. And I believe that their approach was Spirit-inspired. Certainly, all four men would have agreed on the significance of human and spiritual experience in discerning the will of God. But they would have also fully agreed that our ultimate standard is not our experience but the Word of God.

James summarized the argument of the apostles by reminding his audience that the Old Testament prophets agreed with what they were saying: " 'After this I will return and rebuild David's fallen tent. Its ruins I will rebuild, and I will restore it, that the remnant of men may seek the Lord, and all the Gentiles who bear my name, says the Lord . . .' " (Acts 15:16–17, quoted from Amos 9:11–12)

There is no direct statement regarding circumcision per se in this Scripture, but James evidently perceived that God's acceptance of these "outsiders" was not conditioned on their first becoming Jews. And, reasoned James, since Scripture agrees with what we ourselves have witnessed and experienced, "we should not make it difficult for the Gentiles who are turning to God" (v. 19).

How many doctrinal conflicts and divisions would we have if we tested our experiences by the Word of God, rather than tested the Word of God by our experiences? True, many Christians sincerely disagree about interpretations of Scripture. These can be occasions for conflict or occasions for constructive dialog. But I suspect that too many times we search for an interpretation of Scripture to fit our own preconceived ideas rather than honestly let Scripture shape us.

And how many conflicts do we invite because we are more zealous to safeguard our denominational traditions and the homogeneity of our congregations than we are to open our fellowship to all whom God is calling to himself? The overarching truth of the biblical story is that the Father is gathering into one loving fellowship people who are amazingly diverse, who refuse to fit into our neat little categories of judgment and who often have little in common save their simple faith in his son.

5. *Speak the truth in love.* The Holy Spirit has a way of packing dynamite into brief phrases. When Paul reminds us of the importance of "speaking the truth in love" (Eph 4:15), he leaves a time bomb on our doorstep. The admonition sounds harmless enough. After all, isn't everyone—with the exception of chronic liars—in

favor of speaking the truth (at least most of the time!)?

But if we listen closely, we begin to hear an ominous ticking noise emanating from this seemingly innocuous package. We agree with the idea of not lying, of course, but the convicting Spirit of God reminds us that we are skilled in shading the truth. There are ways of gaining an advantage over someone who disagrees with us by putting our own position in the most favorable light while stating our opponent's argument in the least persuasive manner—all without telling an outright lie. We begin to hear that bothersome ticking noise, sounding even louder!

The phrase "in love" is another explosive ingredient. In our better moments, we know that it is all too possible to speak the truth out of a heart filled with bitterness and hatred toward those with whom we contend. Too often we use the truth, not as a means of communication, but as a weapon of destruction aimed not so much at false teaching as at those whose theological understanding is different from ours.

How refreshing, then, to note that in the council at Jerusalem believers managed to express their strong theological convictions in love and to differ with each other without acrimony! It can be done, as the experience of those early Christians reminds us.

I visited a flourishing church in northern New York State, and was deeply impressed by the evidences of growth and fruitfulness. "What has God been doing among you recently?" I asked the pastor. To my surprise, the first thing he cited was not their evangelistic efforts or their attendance statistics. Instead, he told of the working of God in a discussion group to which the congregation was invited after their Sunday evening service.

"Each week the group tackles some current (and controversial) issue," he said. "They focus on relevant biblical teaching on the subject, and then open the meeting for discussion of varying points of view held by the participants in the group."

"Isn't that a daring thing to do?" I wondered. The spectrum of political, social and even religious opinions held by the group's members was a broad one. "Isn't there a risk of bitterness, and even alienation?"

Yes, he admitted, but the group had a deep desire to approach the various issues in the unity of the Holy Spirit. "The Scriptures are normative for the discussions, but where there are differences in interpretation among the group's members, they are learning to listen to one another, learn from each other and open their hearts to further light from God. The group is also learning how varieties of cultural, economic and social backgrounds produce divergent viewpoints. Those positions are allowed full expression."

As I listened in astonishment to some of the issues they had discussed—homosexuality, the roles of men and women, the gifts of the Spirit, the role of Christians in politics, civil disobedience—there didn't seem to be wishy-washy compromise or pulling punches. But there was no rancor either. People expressed their perception of the truth in love, and if no full consensus had been arrived at by the end of the meeting neither had the unity of the church been threatened. I liked the way the pastor summed it all up: "God's Spirit is at work among us. He is even teaching us to enjoy our differences!"

Remember . . .

We dare not settle for admiring the way the early Christians dealt with the grave doctrinal issue that threatened to destroy the church. Surely God means us to learn that *believers are entitled to a full and fair hearing of their case* when they differ with us. And the Jerusalem congregation (which must have been every bit as flawed as your church or mine) reminds us not only to listen to each other, but also to ask basic questions: "How has God dealt with this issue in the past?" and "What are the consequences likely to be of pursuing this or that direction?" Finally, the early church is an example to us to seek our answers in the Scriptures and in our knowledge of how God has worked in our lives and in the lives of his people down through the ages.

Once a conclusion has been reached on the question at hand, however, the process is not over. The war has been won. But the peace can easily be lost if the decisions are not communicated carefully both to those whose views were vindicated and to those whose convictions were overruled. How the council in Jerusalem handled this issue is the topic of the next chapter.

7
When Doctrine Divides (Part 3): Caring for the "Losers"

WHEN THE ARMIES OF THE SOUTH surrendered to General U. S. Grant's forces, bringing the American Civil War to an end, Grant knew that the success of his victory might well depend on dealing graciously, not vindictively, with his defeated foe. His generosity in the terms of surrender was not only commendable, it represented a valiant attempt to initiate the process of healing immediately. And it paid off in the succeeding years. We are the *United* States of America.

Historians point out, in contrast, that the seeds of World War 2 were sown in the months and years immediately following the first world conflict. It's easier to understand the rise of Adolf Hitler and the blood bath into which he plunged the world if we remember the harsh treatment meted out to the vanquished forces of Germany by the powers which triumphed militarily in 1918.

That lesson was learned and applied, in some measure at least, when it came time to establish the peace after World War 2. To be sure, war criminals were prosecuted and many of them were executed or given heavy prison sentences. The cause of justice was not overlooked. But at the same time, the Marshall Plan and other rehabilitative programs were instituted, aimed at the long-term well-being of the conquered nations and the early re-establishment of peaceful relations. The emperor of Japan, for instance, was allowed to continue on the throne even though strict standards of justice might have called for his death. The Allies had learned that the aftermath of victory has a great bearing on the prospects for a continuing peace.

It's possible in our churches to "win the battle but lose the war" when it comes to settling doctrinal disputes. Even when a just cause triumphs, "victory" is not enough. Indeed, with the cessation of hostilities, a new and critical period is entered which may decide how long the peace will last. There are crucial questions to be faced: How are the vanquished to be treated? How are the wounded to be cared for? How is unity to be restored among the opposing forces, and how will it be maintained?

Francis Schaeffer was involved in the doctrinal controversy which racked the northern Presbyterian denomination in the 1930s. In later life he felt that great harm had been done because both sides in the bitter struggle had seemed content to claim "victory" for their cause without giving enough thought as to how the other side was to be treated, either in the heat of the battle or in its aftermath. While maintaining that his group had been right to insist on doctrinal purity, Schaeffer lamented their lack of love for those with whom they differed.

Later, as he looked back on this experience, he expressed his heartache in writing: "All the lines of a practical example of observable love were destroyed. . . . The periodicals of those who left the denomination (and Schaeffer himself had been of that number) tended to devote more space to attacking people who differed with them on the issue of leaving than to dealing with the liberals. Things that were said are difficult to forget even now. Those who came out refused to pray with those who had not come out. Many who left broke off all forms of fellowship with true brothers in Christ who had not left. What was left was frequently a turning inward, a self-righteousness, a hardness. The impression often was left that coming out had made those who departed so right that anything could be excused. Having learned such bad habits, they later treated each other badly when the resulting new groups had minor differences among themselves." Schaeffer then warned in his book, *The Great Evangelical Disaster:* "Beware of the habits we learn in controversy."

Many of us could testify to similar experiences. If, like Schaeffer, we truly desire to repent of these sins and seek the way of Christ in such matters, we could do no better than turn for help to the final episode of the narrative in Acts 15.

Heal the Wounds of Conflict
With James's final judgment that "we should not make it difficult for the Gentiles who are turning to God" (15:19), the Jerusalem council decided the basic issue: the Gentiles should not be required to be circumcised to join the fellowship of believers. James then offered a recommendation for how to proceed: " 'Instead we should write to them, telling them to abstain from food polluted by idols, from sexual immorality, from the meat of strangled animals and from blood. For Moses has been preached in every city from the earliest times and is read in the synagogues on every Sabbath" (vv. 20-21).

1. Minister love to all concerned. The council had not yet finished their task. Now the question was: "How shall our decision
be communicated in a way that is true to our convictions while
at the same time compassionate to those whose position has been
rejected by the council?" In other words, "How can we manifest
our love for all involved?"

That would be no easy task! But James saw it as essential to the
restoration of unity and the preservation of peace in the family.
God had given him the wisdom to include in his "motion" a word
of reassurance to the Gentiles (they were to be received into full
standing in the church without becoming Jews first) and a word
of challenge (they were advised to accept certain limitations on
their lifestyle which the party of the Pharisees would have been
greatly concerned about). In giving this dual message, James resolved the issue that troubled the Gentiles while showing appreciation for the concerns of the Pharasaic Jews whose position had
been rejected by the council. Thus, God's truth about salvation
would be firmly established while the losers in the debate would
know that although their position had been rejected, they had not
been.

What consummate wisdom James showed here! Later in his
epistle he wrote, "If any of you lacks wisdom, he should ask God,
who gives generously to all without finding fault, and it will be
given to him" (Jas 1:5). He was living proof that God hears such
prayers and gladly gives the wisdom his servants so sorely need
in the healing of conflicts.

Certainly in our present-day controversies we desperately need
the same gift! For by now we must be convinced that winning a
battle, however worthy the cause, is not enough. Establishing
peace, in love for both vanquished and victors, is essential to any
victory worthy of the name.

In driving along the highways (of the North as well as the South),

I often see cars displaying the flag of the Confederacy as it was proudly flown by the South during the War between the States. I have no wish to judge the motives of those who continue to fly the banner of rebellion more than a century after that conflict ended. But I find myself wondering how long it will be in the Christian church before we make our unity in Christ the flag we fly rather than the banner of secondary issues which divide us.

2. Communicate in writing and in person. The leaders of the early church were not only concerned about the content of their communication, they also carefully considered how it could best be communicated.

Too much was at stake to risk any breakdown in conveying the important decision they had reached. And so "the apostles and elders, with the whole church, decided to choose some of their own men and send them to Antioch with Paul and Barnabas. They chose Judas (called Barsabbas) and Silas, two men who were leaders among the brothers. With them they sent [a] letter" (Acts 15:22-23).

The council took prudent measures to avoid any possible misunderstanding, by either Gentiles or Jews. They conveyed their convictions in a letter. But they weren't content merely to communicate by means of an official document. They knew that even a carefully prepared statement might raise additional questions in the minds of the Antioch believers, and those would need authoritative and definitive answers. Moreover, they were undoubtedly aware of the importance of supplementing even the best of letters by the warmth of face-to-face contact, sending those who could by word and attitude communicate the loving concern which characterized the decisions reached by the mother church.

There is value for us, centuries later, in the way they went about this! For one thing, it is often essential to put in writing the viewpoints expressed and the conclusions arrived at when resolving a conflict. On occasion, even the minutes of the meeting can be a means of grace! But if a mistake must be made, let it be on the side of too much communication, rather than too little!

How wise it is to also wrap such a document in warm human love, expressed by the messengers who bear the letter! The best of written records may seem cold or harsh, even when its writers never intended it that way. Just as dialog is more helpful in healing breaches than a monolog, so the combination of carefully written communication and human interpretation motivated by love is likely to be much more effective than one used alone.

About thirty years ago, John, a young seminary professor, was sent on sabbatical to get some practical church experience to help temper some of his idealistic views of the church. Along with a few others, he planted a new church in an urban area with a vision to build a real community of faith along the lines of the first church in Acts: "All the believers were one in heart and mind. No one claimed that any of his possessions was his own, but they shared everything they had. . . . Those who owned lands or houses sold them, brought the money from the sales and put it at the apostles' feet, and it was distributed to anyone as he had need" (Acts 4:32–35).

This approach to economics and stewardship, however, unsettled the seminary administrators. They wrote John several concerned letters, outlining their questions, to which he responded. Finally they arranged to visit the little congregation, and many of their concerns were laid to rest in the warmth of face-to-face fellowship. Even though tensions did not entirely disappear between John and the seminary until several years later (he was not reinstated), there was none of the rancor and bitterness which often accompanies a divergence of theological understanding and practice.

When a disciple of Christ is accused of shortcomings or is to be confronted with an action to which he or she is personally opposed, it is only fair that the person be provided with a written statement of the concerns and charges, so that both sides have a chance to come to an understanding of the nature of the problem at issue. But it helps doubly when instead of a continuing exchange of correspondence there can be a frank and loving discussion of the written document. There is no guarantee that using both these approaches will bring a happy ending to the dispute. But certainly we have learned from our experience in families, and as lay leaders in the church or as pastors, that hope of healing is greatly increased when we use every possible way of communicating the truth in love.

3. Don't compromise on basics. We have no record of what the emissaries from Jerusalem said to the assembled saints in Antioch. But we do have the text of the letter which they carried.

The apostles and elders, your brothers, To the Gentile believers in Antioch, Syria and Cilicia: Greetings.

We have heard that some went out from us without our authorization and disturbed you, troubling your minds by what they said. So we all agreed to choose some men and send them to you with our dear friends Barnabas and Paul—men who have risked their lives for the name of our Lord Jesus Christ. Therefore we are sending Judas and Silas to confirm by word of mouth what we are writing. It seemed good to the Holy Spirit and to us not to burden you with anything beyond the following requirements: You are to abstain from food sacrificed to idols, from blood, from the meat of strangled animals and from sexual immorality. You will do well to avoid these things. Farewell. (Acts 15:23-29)

The first emphasis here was that there would be no compromise on the basic issue: No party in the church, however sincere and earnest, could add anything to the gospel of God's grace.

Let's give the party of Pharisee-Christians every benefit of the doubt. They may have feared that this congregation would make entrance into the kingdom too easily, and they may have wanted to raise certain safeguards against "cheap grace." Perhaps they would have paid lip service to the idea that salvation is by faith in Christ alone.

But having said that, they may have insisted that the Gentiles needed to be aware of the seriousness of becoming citizens of the kingdom, and that the requirement of circumcision might help them to realize the necessity of a complete break with their old life. "After all," they may have said, "you don't want to make coming into the Christian church a cheap, meaningless thing, do you?"

The official communication from Jerusalem confronted that question head on, and made it plain that while eternal salvation is not cheap, it is free because it has been fully paid for by the precious blood of Jesus Christ. To add any human ritual as a prerequisite to enjoying the fellowship of God's family is indeed to cheapen not only God's offer of eternal life but also the sacrifice of Christ which has made that offer possible.

Of course we need to be on our guard against making membership in the body of Christ no more than admission to the local country club. Some churches, eager to increase their membership, have lowered their standards in the hope of attracting more people.

But I have personally known evangelical churches who have their own version of Ephesians 2:8 as their requirement for membership: "By grace you have been saved—plus your wholehearted acceptance of our view of eschatology." Granted the importance of the biblical teaching concerning Christ's return, is anyone's entrance into the body of Christ to be made conditional on accepting a particular order of events in prophecy?

I have known churches that banned people from their fellowship not because they weren't trusting Christ but because they were smokers. Granted the truth of the Surgeon General's ominous warnings about the link between smoking and cancer, is God's gift of eternal life contingent on avoiding health-destroying habits?

Having been through my share of stewardship campaigns as a pastor, I confess to envying on occasion those Korean churches who make tithing a condition of church membership. But granted the important biblical principle of proportionate giving and marveling at the distance we've strayed from it, is this to be made a prerequisite for admission to God's family?

To all our well-meaning attempts to provide safeguards to membership in our churches, the Jerusalem saints would say, "Don't subtract anything from God's good news, but don't add to it, either!"

The letter addressed to Antioch certainly insists that there are places where the Christian congregation dares not compromise and that any attempt to compromise on clearly revealed doctrines of Scripture is to head for disaster. The gift of Christian unity is a precious one, but any attempt to maintain it at the cost of surrendering the truth of God means paying too high a price and not getting what you pay for! In such areas, compromise is unthinkable.

4. But be patient on secondary issues. There's a second principle involved in this letter which in some ways is even more difficult to accept. What are we to make of the insistence here that although Gentiles must not be forced to accept circumcision, they were urged to "abstain from food sacrificied to idols, from blood, from the meat of strangled animals and from sexual immorality" (Acts 15:29)? The first three, at least, seem like the very kinds of rules and regulations which can put Christians under bondage!

The apostle Paul told the Colossians, "Do not let anyone judge you by what you eat or drink," and, "Since you died with Christ to the basic principles of this world, why . . . do you submit to its rules: 'Do not handle! Do not taste! Do not touch!' " (Col 2:16, 20–21). But the Jerusalem council seemed in danger of retreating from the high ground they had just taken in rejecting legalism, by making concessions to the law party in the church. Was this a psychological ploy intended to pacify the defeated party? On the face of it, it appeared to be contradictory counsel in which the second admonition neutralized the first.

And what shall we say to the claim that the actions recommended "seemed good to the Holy Spirit and to us" (Acts 15:28)? Surely the Spirit would not grant liberty with one hand and take it away with the other!

But when we examine the situation among the believers of Jerusalem and Antioch, it becomes apparent that they indeed had a wisdom not their own in dealing with this particular case. Compromise it may have been, in one sense. But "compromise" is not always the dirty word we sometimes make it out to be. Indeed, what they did illustrates a principle of conflict management which we might well emulate in dealing with our disagreements.

The thesis of President John F. Kennedy's remarkable book, *Profiles in Courage,* was that under certain circumstances, political compromise is not necessarily a surrender to expediency. Instead, it may be a strategy that is both ethical and useful. It makes sense, he argued, not to press certain secondary issues if victory at a more basic level can be achieved by not trying to fight lesser battles at the same time.

The early church knew as well as we do that obedience to the Lord is the crucial thing, but they clearly felt led not to insist on their freedom to ignore all ceremonial regulations concerning "clean and unclean" foods. Instead, they asked the Gentiles to accept a restraint on their liberty by joining with the apostles in observing some of these regulations, knowing that there was no gain in humiliating the opposition unduly. This was not a retreat to a new legalism. It was an assurance to the losers that the Mosaic laws were not being arbitrarily thrown on the scrap heap. The significance of those regulations could be discussed at a later time. In the meantime they asked the Gentile Christians to make it plain to all that they would have no part of idols, that they would not pollute their bodies which were now temples of the Holy Spirit nor that they would violate rules which had been made for their physical well-being.

Settling disputes between Christians ought never to leave the victors arrogantly triumphant or the losers battered beyond recognition. The strategy of the apostles compels us twentieth-century Christians to ask ourselves some probing questions such as, "How much closer would we be to true unity in Christ today if we were ready to respect the feelings of our vanquished foes and to make concessions to them in areas where our integrity is not compromised by doing so?"

As Francis Schaeffer suggested, we who are eager to defend God's truth, need "to keep consciously before us, and help each other be aware, that if it is easy to compromise, and to call what is wrong right, it is equally easy to forget to exhibit our oneness in Christ."

5. *Seek the mind of Christ.* In claiming that they had been divinely guided in coming to the conclusion reported in their letter (v. 28), the council was not denying their individual or corporate responsibility for the decision they had reached. They had undoubtedly prayed for guidance, and the record shows that they had given much time to discussion of the issue. But as they had done these things, they must also have recalled the assurance that Jesus had given his disciples: "The Holy Spirit . . . will teach you all things and will remind you of everything I have said to you" (Jn 14.26).

They felt that promise had been fulfilled, and they acted only when they shared the conviction that they had been given the mind of the Spirit on this crucial matter.

This was not the Lone Ranger type of guidance so popular today in certain evangelical circles, where some seek to justify their actions by the simple statement, "The Lord told me to do it!" or "I was led by the Spirit to say what I did." Such guidance is rightly suspect, not only by people of the world but by believers who are all too aware of our human fallibility in discovering the will of God. Sometimes our guidance has its roots in presumption and we do well to be aware of that possibility.

But let's not allow our occasional failures in this area to rob us of being truly led by the Spirit! The decision in the letter from Jerusalem hadn't been reached in haste. It hadn't been arrived at by squelching the opposition. Rather, it represented a conscious attempt to seek the mind of Christ as revealed in the written Word and in the experience of servants of God who had been both faithful to the truth as they understood it and were fruitful in their own service for Christ. So the council's confidence that they had come to the right conclusion was based on the fact that God had promised such guidance to his own and that they had carefully, wholeheartedly sought his leading.

Both sides in clashes between Christians need to beware of automatically identifying their own positions, however long and tenaciously held, with the will of God, lest our arrogance verge on a pious form of blasphemy. But if we earnestly and prayerfully seek the will of God, being well aware of the dangers of our own subjectivity, and therefore gladly exposing ourselves to all the available evidence, and if we listen willingly and patiently to Christians who differ with us, we can expect that somewhere along the line God will bring our warring factions to a consensus of which we may say humbly, but with assurance, "It seemed good to the Holy

Spirit and to us." That moment is well worth waiting for and when it comes, we shall move on in the service of God with a strength of conviction and a measure of unity we otherwise would have lacked.

7. Continue to give encouragement. After the delegation from Jerusalem gathered the Antioch believers together and delivered the letter, "the people read it and were glad for its encouraging message. Judas and Silas, who themselves were prophets, said much to encourage and strengthen the brothers" (Acts 15:31-32). In spite of the long and sometimes painful process they'd just been through, the believers were encouraged!

First, they were encouraged by the letter, with its comfort and its challenge. *Encouragement* means "to give courage to." This letter wasn't simply a pat on the back, saying, "Don't worry; everything's fine." It wouldn't be easy to abstain from food offered to idols or to keep themselves from sexual temptation. But they were encouraged to have courage, to keep themselves pure.

I can readily think of three people who have had a tremendous ministry in my life through the encouragement their letters have brought me. All three have had fruitful public ministries and they are very busy people. Yet each finds time, somehow, to write not only to me but also to a host of others—counseling, reproving and encouraging them. Who can measure the effectiveness of such a ministry by correspondence? And what excuse do you and I have for not engaging more fully in this form of service to other Christians, given God's evident readiness to use us in it?

Second, they were encouraged by their visitors, who actually stayed around for awhile before they were "sent off by the brothers with the blessing of peace to return to those who had sent them" (v. 33). The conflict had been stressful so a time of encouragement and upbuilding was important, a ministry which Paul and Barnabas continued after Judas and Silas returned to Jerusalem (v. 35).

102

Remember . . .

So our story has a happy ending, at least as far as this particular doctrinal dispute is concerned. And that's because the church leaders were not only concerned with the issue itself, but how to *heal the wounds of conflict* for all involved. They gave careful thought to communicating their conclusion, both in writing and in the warmth of personal contact. They didn't compromise basic doctrinal truth, but they didn't push their opponents on every issue. They could act in confidence because they sought the mind of Christ in the matter. And they ministered encouragement to those wounded by the conflict.

Antioch's experience provides us with ample assurance that doctrinal disputes don't have to destroy a church. There is a better way! Antioch and Jerusalem found it—and so can your church and mine.

8

Agreeing to Disagree

F OR WEEKS OUR ADULT EDUCATION CLASS had been doing Bible study on the theme which is at the heart of this book: What does God want Christians to do when they clash? We spent almost a month on the passage in Acts 15 which is discussed in the preceding three chapters. The class was encouraged by seeing how the early church resolved their conflict in a way that upheld the truth, their integrity and their unity. Among the class, there was a new spirit of hope that Christian conflicts could be resolved in our own day as well!

Then we studied the last six verses of the chapter. As we reviewed the disagreement between Paul and Barnabas, the spirit of hope in the room changed to despair.

In many ways, I was glad the victory recorded in Acts 15:1-35 was followed by the account of two godly friends coming to an impasse in their relationship. I wanted the class to realize that no matter how many victories we experience, the same stalemate could happen to us. But I was utterly unprepared for the traumatic nature of the class's reaction.

One person expressed the feelings of many others: "When we studied how beautifully the churches in Antioch and Jerusalem met the crisis that threatened to split those groups wide open, I thought there was hope for the church today. But when I read how quickly after that two great leaders like Paul and Barnabas found themselves at loggerheads, the bubble burst!"

What happened to these two apostolic friends so soon after God had used them to help prevent a split in the early church? Nothing less than the possible ending of their own relationship! Let's look at the tragic record:

Some time later Paul said to Barnabas, "Let us go back and visit the brothers in all the towns where we preached the word of the Lord and see how they are doing." Barnabas wanted to take John, also called Mark, with them, but Paul did not think it wise to take him, because he had deserted them in Pamphylia and had not continued with them in the work. They had such a sharp disagreement that they parted company. Barnabas took Mark and sailed for Cyprus, but Paul chose Silas and left, commended by the brothers to the grace of the Lord. He went through Syria and Cilicia, strengthening the churches. (Acts 15:36-41)

Here are two chosen servants of the Lord, each deeply dedicated to the service of Christ, at odds with each other on how their ministry should be carried out! In doctrinal belief, they were one. Moreover they were united in their determination to take Christ's love throughout the world. There was no problem in these crucial areas.

They were also agreed on many of the details concerning their forthcoming trip, including the need to revisit the churches they had planted and the assurance that God would be with them as they earnestly sought to carry out his will. Moreover, they agreed that they needed another team member to accompany them.

But whom to take? To Barnabas, the answer was easy. His cousin John Mark was available and apparently willing to go. Barnabas loved this young servant of Christ and had confidence that he could provide exactly the help they needed. True, Mark had skipped out in the midst of a previous mission, but Barnabas hadn't given up on him and was ready to offer him another chance.

But not Paul! It seemed to him that John Mark had blown his first big opportunity and there was little sense in putting him in a position to fail once again! The mission was too important to risk bringing John Mark along. Paul's response to Barnabas's suggestion was a terse, "No way!"

Suddenly they were worlds apart. Neither one was willing to give in to the other, nor could they find a satisfactory compromise. It looked as though their differences were irreconcilable. Paul and Barnabas were probably shocked themselves at what was happening to their fellowship. For them, too, the bubble had burst.

The two men were at odds over an issue that seemed very important to each of them, and they may have felt that a breakup was inevitable. They finally decided that the only way out was to go their separate ways. Barnabas took John Mark as his traveling companion, while Paul chose Silas. Thus the two who had helped the church at Antioch settle its differences confessed their inability to reconcile their own.

It is not hard to picture James and John (the "Sons of Thunder") having such a disagreement. It would be easy to imagine volatile Peter and opinionated Paul caught up in such a conflict. But Barnabas's name meant "Son of Encouragement" (Acts 4:36) and he had a reputation to match it. And Paul owed his first chance in ministry to Barnabas (11:25). Over time, Paul had come to head up their team, and together they had done so much in Christ's name. How could such a disagreement threaten their joint ministry?

The fact is that it did, and such things happen today as well. I know, because it happened to me.

My friendship with Ken dated back to our college days thirty years before. God had made us colleagues in missionary service in Latin America, and my admiration for him had grown year after year. I loved Ken dearly and was well aware that my love for him was fully reciprocated.

Then it happened. One evening, after we and others in the mission administration had been involved for three days and nights of almost nonstop business sessions, Ken and I found ourselves at odds in an emotionally explosive discussion. The stakes were high. We were discussing how the mission should deal with the leadership of the national churches we had helped bring into being. All involved were dog-tired and past the ability to engage in rational discussion. At this point, Ken and I found ourselves at opposite ends of a particular issue. Sure of the rightness of my position, I dug in my heels and began substituting decibels for reasonable argument. Ken, not much more in control than I, responded in kind. Our co-workers looked on in stunned silence while our verbal battle raged on, unabated.

Our long-standing friendship was forgotten as Ken and I became bitter opponents, each of us privately surprised at how far we had gone and how helpless we felt about halting the argument.

Whoever was at fault (and I'm sure, in retrospect, that it was largely mine), it was evident that what had been previously unthinkable had now come to pass. Our fellowship was broken. We were no longer friends but antagonists.

Ultimately there was a happy ending to the experience. Ken and I asked forgiveness of the other, and it was freely granted. Our fellowship was restored. But for a time, at least, the bubble had burst. After all these years, my memories are fresh enough to keep me from piously wondering how Paul and Barnabas could have found themselves at odds!

Because such things *can* happen, we had better be alert to the lessons which the Holy Spirit wants to teach us from the experience of these first-century Christians.

We Can Agree to Disagree

How could stalwart saints such as Paul and Barnabas come to the parting of the ways? What happened to Ken and me? And if you have had a similar experience with a dear friend, how do you account for it?

The Bible doesn't tell us in explicit detail how Paul and Barnabas came to an impasse. Nor does it pinpoint the blame for their tragic situation. In any case, a serious disruption is seldom the fault of just one person involved. Since little is said, it would seem the Holy Spirit does not want us to judge between the two men. Instead, we should learn what we can from their sad experience and the way they handled it.

1. Accept the fact that differences can happen. The question that remains in our minds is, How could it happen? And while the answer to such a question is always complex—doubly so when the Spirit has not spelled out the answer in great detail—it may still be helpful to grapple with the problem.

If unity is indeed one of the most precious gifts God gives his people, then anything that destroys that unity must be a chief weapon in the Enemy's armory. And if Christ wants us to be one the way that he and his Father are one (Jn 17:22), then Satan must want to undermine our progress toward that goal at any cost. God desires to show the world a unity through Christ that unbelievers can never duplicate. The devil hopes to turn our unity into a laughingstock before the unbelieving world. (Can't you hear their derisive cry, "Even Paul and Barnabas can't get along with each other!"?) How vigilant, then, we ought to be! For the unity God wants us to have in Christ is not optional, not merely "the icing on the cake." It is at the heart of the good news we Christians proclaim.

If persistent Satanic activity is one reason behind the conflicts Christian have, another factor is the humanness of the combatants. We dare not forget that Paul and Barnabas, at their very best, were still fallible human beings—as we are. Scripture clearly teaches this, and our everyday lives bear it out. Even Christians "know in part" (1 Cor 13:12). Our very best judgments are flawed because we lack full perspective on the things we judge. We readily misjudge each other's motives and actions. Even though God will give to those who ask for it a wisdom that is beyond any we could otherwise know (Jas 1:5), we must be humble about our conclusions concerning God's will. We need to question our own motives and arguments because we seldom fully escape the consequences of our humanity. Kenneth Strachan, in his lectures at Fuller Seminary shortly before his death, warned us, "We all need to live and serve in the constant recognition of our own humanity."

Certainly we should not surrender our deep convictions just because they are often challenged by others. But there is something to be said for advancing our arguments against fellow Christians with what one wise man paradoxically called "tentative finality"!

Neither Paul nor Barnabas had the full picture—a fact which need not have silenced them but which should have reminded them of their own fallibility.

The truth is, each man had a strong case. If I had been Paul's supporter, I would have stressed that John Mark had already shown he lacked the perseverance needed for the apostolic calling (Acts 13:13) and that the mission was too important to risk including an unreliable worker. The New Testament warns of our human tendency to quit prematurely and condemns any failure to endure to the end. Why should Paul and Barnabas take a chance on a second defection by this young man?

On the other hand, if I had been called to represent Barnabas, I would readily admit John Mark's earlier failure and chalk it up to his youth, lack of experience in the Lord's work and lack of advance preparation, and the tremendous pressures under which he had been serving. I would remind my hearers of the Christian grace of forgiveness and the need to accompany it with loving restoration. After all, the prodigal son was not given the position of a hired servant on his return to his father's house—regardless of what he deserved! What is the good news but the fact that our failures do not have to be final! What hope is there for *any* of us if we never have the chance to try again?

Both Paul and Barnabas had a valid case, and who of us is to say which was right? Both Ken and I made valid arguments that difficult night, and we each had good reasons for feeling as we did. If you think about it, that is often the case. Different perspectives, different goals, different experiences will lead us to different conclusions, even when brothers and sister share the same basic tenets of our faith.

In a way, differences concerning the tenets of the faith can be easier to handle! As difficult as it was, the issue between the Jewish and Gentile Christians wasn't a *personal* conflict, as the argument between Paul and Barnabas was. Personal conflicts often carry more steam, more emotional weight. Because of this, they *feel* more weighty than broader issues. What may have seemed like a minor point to our co-workers there on the mission field hit me deeply—my friend whom I loved was *disagreeing* with me, challenging me!

Because Satan and our own fallibility make us vulnerable to disagreements, we need to accept the fact that conflicts will arise, even in the closest of relationships. A more important question is, "What do we do when they happen?"

2. Find a temporary solution. Unable to resolve their differences at the moment, Paul and Barnabas decided on a radical remedy, which possibly they recognized was a temporary and incomplete solution: They went their separate ways, forming two missionary teams in place of one. Paul took Silas in place of John Mark; Barnabas honored his conviction about restoring the young man by inviting him to be his traveling partner. The Paul-Barnabas team, so richly blessed in its past service, was broken up for the foreseeable future.

It certainly didn't settle the question of who was "right" about Mark. They decided instead to agree to disagree, a sort of détente, which for the time being allowed each of them to act on his convictions.

Of course, such a decision did not really settle anything—or mend the break in unity between Paul and Barnabas. But it bought time for the two to more thoroughly seek the Lord's will in the matter, and that is no small thing. The basic causes of the conflict were not resolved, but in an imperfect world, filled with imperfect people, it may sometimes be necessary to settle for a solution that seems less than perfect.

In the international arena, détente provides at best an uneasy peace, a situation with which neither of the conflicting parties dares be fully satisfied. But such an incomplete resolution is usually better than continued warfare. And among Christians, such a solution might at least buy time, during which the warring parties may continue in some measure to serve the Lord, while they seek

God's guidance for resolving their differences.

This was the case with Ruth and Gladys, two of my colleagues in Latin America. Both were earnest Christians, capable and gifted missionaries. But when they were assigned to the same department, although with very different responsibilities, they found themselves in constant conflict with each other. They disagreed on administrative procedures and other important aspects of how the work should be carried out. Neither was completely without fault, and each could make a good case for her own position. But they were soon feuding with each other almost constantly, and the usefulness of their service—and the department in which they worked—was in jeopardy. Because their work was continually in the public eye, their bickering was a scandal to unbelievers and believers alike.

In counseling with each of them, I held doggedly to an idealistic principle that was deeply ingrained in me: as believers they ought to get along together, with the Lord's help, and they were obligated as his servants to do so. I tried vainly to help each of them see the other's point of view and to rise above their personal prejudices and their obvious dislike for each other. I prayed with them individually and together. I reasoned with them, tried to show loving patience with them and sought to remind them of the harm they were doing to the work of the Lord. In desperation I even confronted them with the possibility that their missionary careers might have to be terminated.

Nothing worked! Eventually, I was forced to forego my idealism. These women, I decided, would have to be separated. I reassigned Gladys to a responsible position in a different ministry, a position which would not bring the two women into daily contact.

I didn't like this "solution." It was contrary to what I had been telling them about their Christian responsibility to work out their differences right where they were. I felt that they should triumph in the midst of the situation, not flee from it.

But my ideal had not been realized. And so I put distance between these two feuding saints in the hope that they might later be helped to a more satisfying resolution of their conflict. After all, if Paul and Barnabas couldn't get along together . . .

In retrospect, I can see I did the right thing, even though the resolution was less satisfactory than I had hoped for. It sometimes requires time—and space—for the saints to get over their disagreements. If our sanctification were total, this would not be so, but because we mature gradually, there may be a need for "interim arrangements" in settling some of our conflicts.

In my marital counseling, it is only with great reluctance that I ever recommend the temporary separation of a Christian couple, but I recognize that some situations can be helped by such a drastic step. Sometimes each of the partners hears God speak more clearly in the peaceful atmosphere brought about by their temporary separation.

And sometimes, agreeing to disagree may be the best solution of all! Jim and Betsy Brown were a pastoral couple who often opened their home to single adults and single parents and their children. They became a family to those who needed daily support. Minnie, a brand-new Christian who had fled an abusive husband, and her six-year-old daughter, Sarah, were invited to become part of the household.

For awhile things went well. Minnie appreciated support with parenting, and Sarah seemed to thrive in the stable environment. But after a year and a half, Minnie began to resent and resist fitting into the Brown household. Tensions developed between the three adults, especially when Minnie refused to have Sarah follow the same rules and discipline the Brown children lived with.

Jim and Betsy decided it was time for Minnie to move out. Minnie felt rejected and wanted to stay, stating that two families should be able to coexist even if they have differing expectations. Other church staff members also encouraged the Browns to try to work it out. Jim and Betsy felt confused about what to do. Were they being too authoritative as the leaders? Were they wrongly imposing their family rules on Minnie and Sarah?

Then Jim realized that the issue was not who is right and who is wrong. This issue was a difference in family styles. The problem was created by trying to stay together beyond the point of the plan's usefulness. It was OK to disagree on what was best for the kids—but not under the same roof. Jim insisted that Minnie needed to move out, not because she was wrong, but because they needed the freedom to agree to disagree.

The separation was painful, especially for the children, who had grown close. Minnie reluctantly found an apartment for herself and Sarah and continued in the church. But after time had healed some of the feelings of loss, all involved came to understand that it had been exactly the right thing to do. Minnie realized that even as a single parent she wanted to develop her own family identity, and this was more likely apart from the Brown household. Betsy and Minnie also became friends in a new way when they were freed from some of the competition that had developed between them. Agreeing to disagree, while painful at the moment, was the best solution after all.

3. Look for healing in the long run. Apparently, the separation between Paul and Barnabas eventually proved to be healing, whether or not it was the ideal solution to their problem at the time. The work of the gospel was not interrupted and their fellowship with each other, though admittedly under strain, was not permanently destroyed. Indeed, it is worth noting that *two* teams went out spreading the gospel, instead of the one originally contemplated. And time was bought until there could be a complete reconciliation between the two men.

Nevertheless, any attempt to settle differences between Christians merely by separating the antagonists ought to be considered an "interim arrangement" rather than a solution—a halting step toward some better way of resolving the conflict, a chance to better understand the situation by providing the more objective viewpoint that sometimes only comes with time.

We have reason to believe that Paul and Barnabas indeed were reconciled, thank God! It is surely significant that Paul came to write to Timothy, "Get Mark and bring him with you, because he is helpful to me in my ministry" (2 Tim 4:11)! We are not told what had happened since the two men parted, but we may infer that either Paul had changed or John Mark had changed or they both had, for now Paul was seeking the aid of the very man whose service he had once rejected! Whatever had happened, Paul was willing to change his mind about Mark. He didn't try to hold onto his former opinion, just to remain "right."

Paul's later references to Barnabas are equally encouraging. There seemed to be no lingering bitterness between the two men. Instead, Paul later referred to Barnabas as though they were once again co-workers for Christ (1 Cor 9:6; Gal 2:11-13).

Two strongly opinionated men, who had differed so greatly that they allowed a productive partnership to end, apparently were fully reconciled—another instance of the Spirit's persistence in reuniting Christians. It's a sign of hope for all of us, as we wonder how healing can be brought to our own troubled relationships.

Indeed, there is no way to explain the happy ending in this story except to recognize it as the work of the Spirit of God. The Spirit is the author of unity among God's people, and he is grieved when we allow that unity to be destroyed. It is obvious to me that both Paul and Barnabas were Spirit-filled men. Undoubtedly they remained sensitive to the Holy Spirit and allowed him to smooth the rough places between them. And when we allow the Spirit of God to have his way with us, the yawning chasms formed by our differences with each other *can* be bridged, even when it takes some time.

There was also a happy ending to the story of the two missionaries who had to be separated. I can't report that Ruth and Gladys ever became a team with the fullness of love for each other that characterized the relationship of Paul and Barnabas. But I can tell you that both of them became fruitful workers in their new assignments, and that they seemed to develop a healthy respect and love for each other that had been sadly missing in their earlier experience. Surely God was pleased!

Remember . . .

The restored relationship between the first-century saints means that there is hope for you and me—and there *will* be a time when hope will seem like a huge challenge. Reconciliation in such cases doesn't always come easily or quickly. Sometimes we will need to *agree to disagree*. Intermediate steps may need to be taken, and time must be allowed to initiate the healing process that will help us uncover the causes of disunity.

And I venture to say that where differing convictions have been passionately held, reunion may be costly. We may need to let go of a former opinion or acknowledge that we acted hastily. But admitting our errors is a small price to pay for restored relationships.

But the case of Paul and Barnabas is our reminder that with God all things *are* possible. Our differences need not destroy a relationship that is ours through the blood of Jesus Christ. And somehow, in the meantime, a sovereign God sees that his work gets done!

9

When Confrontation Is Necessary

P AUL TANGLING WITH BARNABAS over John Mark's usefulness was
one thing. But what shall we say about Paul taking on Peter, an
acknowledged leader in the early church, over a glaring inconsistency in his conduct? And Paul confronted him not in a private
tête-à-tête but before the other key leaders of the church! It
looked for all the world like a classical case of an irresistible force
meeting an immovable body. Whatever the outcome, we can be
sure that there were shock waves throughout the entire church as
a result of the confrontation.

Paul himself told the story of what happened:

When Peter came to Antioch, I opposed him to his face, because
he was clearly in the wrong. Before certain men came from
James, he used to eat with the Gentiles. But when they arrived,

he began to draw back and separate himself from the Gentiles because he was afraid of those who belonged to the circumcision group. The other Jews joined him in his hypocrisy, so that by their hypocrisy even Barnabas was led astray.

When I saw that they were not acting in line with the truth of the gospel, I said to Peter in front of them all, "You are a Jew, yet you live like a Gentile and not like a Jew. How is it, then, that you force Gentiles to follow Jewish customs? (Gal 2:11-14)

Before going into the details of the story, we should note that there were occasions in apostolic times when it seemed that outright confrontation was called for in dealing with a divisive issue. Nobody valued the unity of the church more than Paul, but it is evident that he wasn't a peace-at-any-price man who would go to any length to avoid conflict if he knew that basic issues were at stake. Such questions couldn't be ducked, and they wouldn't settle themselves. To evade them would mean a compromise of the truth which could only bring disaster to the church.

This is a principle which we ignore at great peril. Some of us twentieth-century Christians, starting with an admirable love for peace in the church, eventually become indifferent; we hate fighting so much that we wind up finding nothing worth fighting for. We so studiously avoid confrontation that we soon discover ourselves tolerating that which God hates. We may buy a brief period of peace and quiet by looking the other way, but sooner or later, we will have to face the fact that we paid too high a price for it. The Bible warns us that there are times when confrontation is in the best interest of all concerned, and Paul's bold step of calling his fellow apostle on the carpet was one of them.

The Accusation
The charge was a serious one. Paul accused Peter of inconsistency in conduct, a devastating charge to make against an acknowl-

edged leader. Indeed, *inconsistency* may not be the right word. Paul was really charging his colleague with hypocrisy. For Peter had enjoyed fellowship with the Gentiles, a cardinal sin in the eyes of the circumcision group. It was a bold position for Peter to take, and if he had maintained it, Paul would have praised him for it. But when some of James's disciples came on the scene, Peter apparently feared their opinion, perhaps afraid of the report they would take back to James. So he surrendered a high principle for a cheap expediency and withdrew from further fellowship with people who were greatly in need of it.

To Paul, this was no small thing. He saw Peter as a trumpet giving an uncertain sound which could only bring sorrow to the gentile believers, false comfort to the legalists and confusion to an unbelieving world which needed a clear witness to the universal outreach of God's love in Christ. To Paul, this meant "not acting in line with the truth of the gospel" (Gal 2:14). He dared not let it pass unchallenged. The situation was a call to confrontation.

Paul's argument was not a theoretical one: he based it on what they had already experienced. They had known the power of the gospel to demolish the walls separating Jews and Gentiles. And in a vision, Peter himself had received clear evidence that God would not require the Gentiles to submit to Jewish ceremonial law in order to become part of God's family (Acts 10:9-48). That issue, Paul supposed, had been settled once and for all by the Council at Jerusalem in the decision we previously studied in the chapters based on Acts 15. Peter, he asserted, should have seen the issue as one which was not to be compromised to please James or anyone. Staying in the good graces of Christians like James was not the question here. It was a matter of obedience to what had "seemed good to the Holy Spirit and to us" (Acts 15:28).

Paul then pointed out that, as is usually the case, hypocrisy always breeds more hypocrisy. "The other Jews joined [Peter] in his hypocrisy, so that by their hypocrisy even Barnabas was led astray" (Gal 2:13). Peter had such influence that others joined him in pretending that they didn't eat with Gentiles either.

Peter should have known that God himself hates hypocrisy, having witnessed the solemn judgment which the Lord meted out to Ananias and Sapphira. The couple had agreed together to sell some land, keep some of the money for themselves, but pretend to give it all to the needs of the church (Acts 5:1-11). Had their lie against the Holy Spirit not been quickly dealt with (they were both struck dead), the practice of hypocrisy would have spread like cancer throughout the body of Christ, with spiritually lethal effects. To Paul, Peter's actions were a summons to confrontation: not a pleasant task but a necessary one. To his credit, Paul did what had to be done, and his example surely is meant to say something to us today.

The Defense Rests
It's always been puzzling to me, a layman as far as the law is concerned, to understand a legal tactic which is occasionally invoked in court trials: after the judge and jury have heard lengthy presentations by prosecution witnesses, a defense lawyer rises to announce, "The defense rests"—without calling any witnesses to the stand! The attorney's motives for doing so may, of course, be varied. Sometimes it seems to imply that the prosecution has presented such a weak case that it's not worthwhile to take the court's time to answer it. It may, on other occasions, be a silent admission of guilt on the part of the defendant or an effort to avoid the kind of cross-examination that would destroy the credibility of any witnesses the defense would call. A trial lawyer could probably give a number of other reasons for adopting this tactic.

In Peter's case, we have no record of any defense he made of the actions Paul criticized. It's hard to believe that Paul would have omitted Peter's reply if he had made one. Certainly it is a principle of justice that the accused has a right to his day in court. Peter's apparent silence here is puzzling, to say the least.

Later on we will analyze that silence. But for now, we will focus our attention, not on the question of Peter's guilt or innocence, but on the fact that confrontation was called for.

Paul did not evade what he felt was a God-given responsibility. This story reminds us that serious issues must be faced, even at the risk of disruption in the church. And, given the fact that the ministries—and fellowship—of Peter and Paul continued to thrive after the confrontation, it certainly appears that Paul's rebuke of his brother in Christ, however harsh it may have seemed to some, was not in vain.

Confront in Obedience and Love

God may ask us to confront another brother or sister in Christ at some point, similar to the difficult task he gave Paul on this occasion. I do not want to give anyone the impression, however, that such an assignment is ever easy or enjoyable. In fact, if we ever relish the thought of confrontation, we are already in big trouble!

Jim is a relatively new Christian who turns to me occasionally for counsel. I have great admiration for him. He has grown tremendously in the few years since he came to know Christ and has shown strong potential for leadership in the group of believers where he has found a spiritual home. We live many miles apart, but he recently paid me a surprise visit. I was blessed by his fellowship and his evident growth since our last time together. But in the midst of our conversation, he remarked eagerly: "You know, Dr. Fenton, I believe that God has given me the special gift of rebuking other believers who are going on the wrong path."

I surely don't know Jim well enough to discern his gifts fully, but something in the way he expressed himself made me squirm.

Though he seemed delighted with his newly adopted role, I sensed
a lack of discretion and tenderness as he told me of his forthright
rebukes of believers who seemed to me to be far more experienced and mature Christians than he was.

"Do you ever consult others before you rebuke someone?" I
asked.

"Not really," he answered casually. "I just follow the prompting
of the Spirit that I should talk to someone."

"How much time do you spend checking out the facts?" I
probed.

"Well, there aren't usually 'facts' in that sense," he explained. "If
I sense that someone has a spirit of greed or is not walking close
to the Lord, I rebuke them in Jesus' name to get it straightened
out."

"How do you follow up your rebuke?" I questioned.

He seemed confused. "Follow up? My job is to call the error to
their attention. Then it's up to them to respond to the conviction
of the Holy Spirit."

I was uncomfortable about Jim's attitude and told him so. I
shared with him the counsel I had received from a well-known
evangelist. He had stressed the great danger involved in announc-
ing God's judgments upon people if our condemnation is not accompanied by great love for them and by genuine heartbreak over
their plight. We prayed together, and I asked God to give Jim great
sensitivity in this area. I have also tried to pray for him faithfully
ever since. We all need to beware lest we too readily adopt the role
of judge of others, not only pronouncing our verdict on their conduct, not only deciding their guilt, but executing our judgment on
them as well.

Instigating a confrontation is always a tough role. While the goal
of the process may commend itself, it is not likely that the process
itself will be of any joy to us. In fact, many of us are so dismayed

by shoot-from-the-hip confronters like Jim that we tend to maintain a traitorous silence rather than speak up in the face of error.

To prepare ourselves for the possible need to confront another believer, we should answer a few questions: What does it take to confront a fellow believer effectively? How should we approach such a task? What should our attitude be? What should we do to make it a helpful, rather than a damaging, experience? Paul's confrontation of Peter may give us some guidelines.

1. Be sure the task is yours. One gets the impression that Paul was not acting on a sudden impulse when he called his fellow apostle to account. In fact, Paul was uniquely qualified to confront Peter about his hypocrisy. In the early verses of Galatians 2, Paul gave some background on the issue: how he had tested out his call with James, Peter and John and received their blessing to take the gospel to the Gentiles (vv. 1-10); how he and Barnabas had been commissioned to bridge the centuries-old chasm between Jew and Gentile. When Paul confronted Peter, he realized he was the obvious person to speak up; he had both the credentials and the experience to know what he was talking about.

Unlike Jim, I'm not at all sure that God ever gives someone the ongoing job of confrontation, asking that person to go around confronting people. Rather, I believe that confrontation is a specific task God may ask any of us to do when our responsibility in a situation or our relationship with a person makes us right for the job. It's not only a task for leaders, however. God may ask a lay person to confront an elder or pastor, a friend to confront a friend, a staff member to confront another co-worker. We must learn the difference between confronting on impulse when we don't happen to like something and responding to the leading of the Holy Spirit.

2. Investigate the charges thoroughly. When Paul confronted Peter, he did not make charges based on unconfirmed rumors about Peter's behavior. Like Paul himself, Peter had been acting in freedom among the Gentiles, supporting the good news that conforming to the law was no longer the basis for fellowship between Jews and Gentiles. Paul himself observed Peter's change in behavior when the disciples of James arrived. Suddenly Peter separated himself from the Gentiles so as not to offend those of the circumcision party.

Paul was right in the midst of the controversy. Fellow believers were following Peter's poor example—even Barnabas was being led astray. In all probability, some of the gentile believers also came to Paul, saying, "What's going on?" This scenario was happening in Paul's own back yard. It affected his own partner in ministry as well as the gentile believers. Paul decided to speak up "[w]hen I saw that they were not acting in line with the truth of the gospel . . ." (Gal 2:14). His charges were based not on hearsay but firsthand experience.

3. Confront with courage. It takes more than assurance of the rightness of your cause, however, to initiate a confrontation. A tremendous measure of courage is also demanded.

The steps Paul took were motivated by the strong conviction that Peter was guilty of a sin that Paul dared not leave unchallenged (Gal 2:11). Paul was willing to be Peter's accuser, but only because he was convinced that there was so much at stake for both his beloved colleague and the church itself, and that a confrontation, however painful, could not be postponed.

Humanly speaking, there are great risks involved in taking such a step, and no doubt Paul was aware of them before he confronted Peter. Paul, who once characterized himself as the "chief of sinners," deeply admired the man he had to confront. By confronting, Paul might destroy their warm relationship. It was a courageous act for a person who valued his friendships highly. Only God could have given that kind of courage.

4. Confront in love. Even more than courage, a God-given love is required of anyone who would undertake such a mission. Before any of us try to call a fellow Christian to account, we had better be sure of our own motives in doing so. If our purpose is to take others down a peg or two, or to contrast their faults with our own righteousness, we had better abstain from the ministry of correction. Though no one's motives can ever be spotlessly "pure," our overriding motivation should be the love of Christ.

Maybe Paul had his confrontation with Peter in mind when he wrote to the Galatians, "Brothers, if someone is caught in a sin, you who are spiritual should restore him gently. But watch yourself, or you also may be tempted. Carry each other's burdens, and in this way you will fulfill the law of Christ" (Gal 6:1-2). What is the point of confronting a brother in sin? To restore him. How do we do it? Gently, knowing we too are often in need of rebuke. What does it mean to carry each other's burdens? To hang in there through the process, until restoration is complete. What is the law of Christ we fulfill in this kind of redemptive confrontation? The law of love.

This is love! To confront and restore can be the most loving thing we can do—if we do it in the Spirit of Christ. I think it was this sort of love I missed in my friend Jim's proud accounts of his exploits in rebuking other Christians.

One day I watched a colleague of mine face the prospect of confrontation. Among Jack's administrative responsibilities was overseeing one of our choicest missionaries, who, surprisingly enough, created some serious problems for the mission.

This man, whom I'll call Harry, was in charge of an important department for our mission, and God had blessed him with a lot of creativity and energy. However, in his zeal to try out new ideas or get a job done, he regularly ignored administrative channels, often with the best of intentions and with a warmth that disarmed the rest of us for a time. He was generous. If there weren't enough funds for a project dear to his heart—such as a literature-publishing program—he'd pay for it himself, out of a legacy he had received from his mother's estate. But again and again he launched projects that conflicted with established mission policy and created problems in other departments. He would often announce policies that conflicted with other ministries, without consulting their leaders or his own supervisors. Sometimes no great harm was done, but increasingly Harry became a major problem in the work, until the situation became intolerable.

When Jack came to the reluctant conclusion that Harry would have to be confronted, he asked me to sit in on the interview. Both of us faced the occasion with great trepidation and much prayer. It wasn't going to be a pleasant thing to do, given our love for Harry and the fruitfulness of some aspects of his ministry. But the confrontation was essential to the overall good of the work and to Harry's future usefulness with the mission.

As we had anticipated, the interview was anything but easy. I watched as Jack carried out his difficult task, marveling at the way God had provided the gifts of love, clarity and firmness Jack needed to bring it to a fruitful conclusion. It was evident to me that Jack had prepared carefully for his task, not only by seeking God's help through prayer, but also by digging out the facts that supported the charges he was making. The evidence he cited was not based on hearsay or rumor. It was thoroughly documented.

Moreover, it was evident that Jack had carefully weighed the costs of confrontation and had the courage to go ahead despite whatever risks were involved for Harry or for the mission we served. It would have been easy to postpone the interview indefinitely, hoping that the situation would somehow improve without such a risky intervention. It must have been apparent to Harry, as it was to me, that it took God-given courage for Jack to confront him.

Best of all, Jack demonstrated a special kind of love for Harry in calling him to account—the kind that only God can put in our hearts. He showed no delight in calling a co-worker on the carpet. He expressed a deep concern for Harry's best interests, as well as for those of the mission. He experienced no joy in censuring a colleague but rather demonstrated a deep desire to enable Harry to have an even more fruitful ministry than he had previously known. The outcome of all this was a real triumph—but more about that later!

I am aware that my own ministry has often failed in this area. Writing this chapter brought to mind a few glaring examples of occasions when, for lack of courage or love, I failed to confront a fellow believer for whom I had some responsibility. Having confessed my failures to God, and having asked not only for forgiveness but also for his gracious action in redeeming those failures, I don't want to wallow in continuing self-reproach. But, challenged by the examples of leaders like Paul and Jack, I hope I will be willing to act when confrontation is needed, if I truly have the interests of the kingdom of God at heart.

5. *Profit from being confronted.* If it's difficult to lovingly, courageously confront a fellow Christian, it's just as hard—or harder—to be on the receiving end! I certainly don't enjoy having my character or conduct criticized, or being told that I'm not measuring up to expectations. At first, I am usually defensive: "This person has wronged me," or, "I'm being judged unfairly." I am likely to respond with a hurt silence or an angry retort. Inwardly I take the offensive by attacking the motives or the methods of the one who has confronted me (on the theory that the best defense is a good offense!). It doesn't help much to remember that most of God's servants have had similar experiences and that some reacted the same way I have.

As a young man, I had just been called to pastor a fine church, and I was feeling pleased with my new situation. In a magnanimous mood, I asked the elders to please share with me any suggestions they had concerning how I could improve my ministry. I hope I was being honest and not merely fishing for compliments! In any case, my motives were not severely tested during my "honeymoon" with the congregation. Most of the comments in that period *were* compliments, and I loved it!

Then one night, one of the elders caught me off guard. "I have a suggestion about your sermons," he began. I must have looked startled because he hastily assured me, "Oh, they're fine in most respects. But they're too long. Several of us think their impact would be much improved if you would cut each one by at least five or ten minutes."

I was both hurt and angry. Did the elders have any idea how long and hard I worked preparing those sermons? Inwardly I sputtered that obviously the *Lord* wasn't offended by their length since many had told me my messages had brought great blessing to their hearts. I wanted to remind the elders that they never seemed to mind sitting on hard benches for two or three *hours* to watch a baseball or football game! Why should they demand shorter sermons? Besides, didn't they know that, as one preacher observed, "Sermonettes make Christianettes"?

In retrospect, I'm not at all proud of my reactions, even though I didn't actually voice them. I see now that my self-defense was clear evidence of spiritual immaturity on my part. But I went away from that meeting convinced that my ministry wasn't really appreciated and asking the Lord to deliver me from having to minister further to such ungrateful people.

I hope that through the ensuing years I have been able to see such confrontations not as malicious attacks on my character, but rather as opportunities to learn something about myself and how I can serve the Lord better. Slowly I began realizing that when I listen to my critics, I often learn how to be more effective in the work of Christ.

I can't claim an unbroken string of victories in my responses since then, but I am encouraged by the ways God has used some of those confrontations to greatly enrich me. Not too long ago, I was feeling swamped by my work. Wanting desperately to be delivered from it all, I shared my feelings with a close friend. Dave listened to me sympathetically, and when I was all done pouring out my woes, he said, "I don't think you're overwhelmed because your work schedule in itself is too heavy."

"What do you mean?" I asked defensively, thinking that that was precisely the problem!

"Well," he said carefully, "I think the root of the problem is something you need to work on. You want people to have a good opinion of you, and you are so fearful of disappointing those who have high expectations of you, that you say yes to every invitation for service that comes your way! You don't really look to the Lord for wisdom in discerning which of these assignments the Lord means for you to take."

Bull's eye! A few smart answers flashed through my mind, but there was also a nagging suspicion inside me that Dave was right. I struggled with accepting his analysis of the problem, but I knew that it took courage for him to speak so honestly with me, and that he would only do so because he had my good at heart. The Holy Spirit confirmed within me what Dave had said and taught me a lesson about myself that I needed to learn—and keep on learning. I think I was helped in the process by remembering how Peter responded to Paul's rebuke.

Granted that, as we've already noted, the Bible is strangely silent as to how Peter did react, and I don't want to be guilty of reading too much into that silence. But we have no indication whatever that their fellowship was blighted, even temporarily, by this experience. Nor do we ever again find Peter accused of inconsistency or hypocrisy. I believe this is because Peter accepted the rebuke and learned from it. If this reading is correct, we may thank God for a fellow believer who learned to profit from criticism, to admit his failings when they are called to his attention and to grow in any way that would increase his usefulness for God.

That's the way the confrontation between Jack and Harry came out. It was difficult for Harry to hear, but he fully acknowledged the truth of the charges made against him, asked the Lord's forgiveness and sought God's help in dealing with the problem. He agreed to be accountable to Jack, not only by using established administrative channels in the course of his daily work but by reviewing his progress with Jack from time to time. The habit of charging ahead wasn't easy to break, but Harry was now aware of the problem, and when an incident was called to his attention, he acknowledged the problem right away and took steps to rectify the situation. As would be expected, his effectiveness as a servant of Christ increased!

Remember . . .

There is no bargain-basement price on settling disputes between Christians. It will never be an easy assignment to confront another believer because God tells you to do so, and because you love that Christian and the cause of Christ. Indeed, our motives are suspect, as I've already noted, if we ever find pleasure in initiating such a confrontation. The one who does it in the Spirit of Christ will usually experience heaviness of heart in facing the task. The ministries of correction and reconciliation are costly, not the least to the one who calls another to account.

Nor is it easy to be the one who is the object of another Christian's concern. The confrontation may, at least for the moment, make the person feel like the defendant in a court trial. But the man or woman who receives such a rebuke in good spirit, desiring to learn from it, is likely to experience wonderful consequences as his or her effectiveness for Christ is enlarged and strengthened.

10

The Blessed
Role of
Peacemaker

BLESSED ARE THE POOR in spirit," Jesus said in his mountainside sermon, "the ones who are sorry for their sins . . . the gentle and humble . . . those who show mercy to others . . . who desire righteousness more than food and water. . . ."

Does this sound like the average role model in America today? Hardly. We have Masters of the Universe casting a spell on mesmerized preschoolers Saturday morning . . . J. R. Ewing, on the TV show "Dallas," stepping on anyone who gets in his way . . . Calvin Klein unabashedly selling his jeans with sexy ads . . . and television preachers assuring their viewers, "God wants you rich!"

No, the "blessed" people Jesus was talking about do not get much media coverage. And this is true for another quality that Jesus emphasized: "Blessed are the peacemakers, for they will be called sons of God" (Mt 5:9).

When we think of peacemakers, maybe we think about states-men and negotiators, grappling with the problems caused by con-flicting national ambitions, nuclear proliferation, and oppressed peoples crying out for justice throughout the world. And rightly so! For if these issues cannot be resolved peaceably, there seems to be little hope for the continued survival of our planet.

But do Christ's words apply only to those who sit around inter-national conference tables? Of course not. We who claim the name of Jesus are called to be peacemakers in our homes, where we work, and in our churches, calling each other to be reconciled to God and to one another. Paul said, "All this is from God, who reconciled us to himself through Christ and *gave us the ministry of reconciliation"* (2 Cor 5:18, italics mine).

If Christians are really called to a ministry of reconciliation be-tween humanity and God, that ministry must include building bridges between groups and individuals who are at war with each other. Otherwise, the gospel of Jesus Christ becomes a stumbling block to those who are asking, "What difference does the power of God make in your lives? You say you have peace with God, so why don't you have peace among yourselves?"

The role of peacemaker is not always an attractive one. If we come upon two people in conflict, our first instinct is to stay out of it! It's hard enough handling our own battles, let alone getting involved in those of others. We need assurance that the humble ministry of reconciliation is worth the effort, that it is important to the work of the kingdom and that we're not just sticking our nose in someone else's business.

The Holy Spirit gives us this assurance by recounting an attempt Paul made to reconcile two believers whose conflict threatened the joy and effectiveness of the Philippian church. As Paul brought his letter to this little church to a close, he made some personal remarks: "I plead with Euodia and I plead with Syntyche to agree with each other in the Lord. Yes, and I ask you, loyal yokefellow, help these women who have contended at my side in the cause of the gospel, along with Clement and the rest of my fellow workers, whose names are in the book of life" (Phil 4: 2-3).

Trouble Brewing

The believers at Philippi had experienced a remarkable degree of unity, as well as faith and generosity. The apostle Paul wrote them a letter expressing the great joy they gave him and celebrating the Philippian church's growth in the things of Christ.

But trouble lurked beneath the surface in this seemingly peaceful church. Two of its members, Euodia and Syntyche, evidently had had a falling-out. We know nothing of the controversy except that these two were at odds with each other. To some, the situation may not have seemed very threatening. After all, any time you get a heterogeneous group together (note that the Philippian church had as its charter members a rich businesswoman, an ex-slave girl who had been demon-possessed, and a hardened jailer!), you are bound to have some disagreements. So if two of the members could not get along, what is so unusual or threatening about that?

Paul did not see it that way. Apparently he felt there was danger to the church and its witness in letting the conflict continue. As J. A. Motyer put it in his *Philippian Studies: The Richness of Christ:* "Where there is agreement as to what the Gospel is and what ought to be done with it, there is no room left for personal disagreement. . . . Where Christians cannot bear the sight of each other they will not be able to look the world in the face, either."

Motyer's words are not too strong. I have seen members of one congregation, in which there was no real doctrinal disagreement, argue about whether the pastor or the board of elders had the final say in matters of church policy. They reached the place where they truly seemed to hate each other. A few persons turned from the original issue and began petty personal quarrels. Their biting and snapping not only destroyed each other but made their congregation a spectacle to other believers and a laughingstock to cynics and skeptics in the unbelieving world. All because they allowed differences between them to become the occasion for vicious personal conflict.

Because conflicts between individual members *do* affect the church as a whole, they call for people willing to be peacemakers. But where does a peacemaker begin?

Create a Positive Context for Peacemaking

Paul saw Euodia's and Syntyche's controversy as a potential threat to the congregation, and hence a call to action. There could be no temporizing. Result: We have here a beautiful picture of a peacemaker at work. His mode of action carries timeless lessons for us, lessons not only on dealing promptly with cancerous conflicts but on the actual therapy to use.

1. Consider the whole forest . . . There's a favorite object lesson teachers employ. You take a clean sheet of paper and put a small black dot in the middle.

"What do you see?" you ask.

"A black dot," will be the answer.

It's easy to understand why students fail to say, "A white sheet of paper." When something is amiss, all of us tend to zero in on the problem. It's like being so close to the trees that we fail to see the forest.

Note that Paul didn't begin his letter to the Philippians by pinpointing the problem. He devoted the first three-quarters of his letter to his great joy over the life and witness of this congregation. He affirmed before he corrected. I doubt Paul was merely practicing good psychology. I think he meant it. But at the same time, he created an atmosphere of gratitude and love, and in doing so provided a context in which his words of rebuke could be more readily received. (And that *is* good psychology!) In a similar way the Lord, in sending messages to the seven churches of Asia Minor (Rev 2:1—3:22), found much to affirm in these weak and struggling groups. He expressed his delight in them before he called them to account for their failings.

Paul also began his letter by reminding the believers how much God had done for them. He knew that all of us are more likely to deal kindly with each other's failings when we remember how graciously God has dealt with us. Jesus taught that the person who has been forgiven much will love much (Lk 7:42-43, 47). And in another epistle, Paul encouraged the Ephesian Christians to "Be kind and compassionate to one another, forgiving each other, just as in Christ God forgave you" (Eph 4:32).

Also note how Paul stressed the importance of unity in the church long before he dealt with the specific situation that threatened that unity. He urged the whole church to "stand firm in one spirit" (Phil 1:27); to contend against the Enemy as one man (1:27); to be like-minded, to have the same love, and to be one in spirit and in purpose (2:2). These were exhortations the whole congregation needed to hear, not just the two quarreling women. He wanted the entire group to see how Christians should relate to each other, so that they might see that unresolved conflict among them was scandal to the world and highly displeasing to God.

2. . . . But don't beat around the bush. Paul did not postpone confronting the problem indefinitely. If there was wisdom in dealing with other things before bringing up the conflict between Euodia and Syntyche, he also refused to tiptoe around this particular threat to the church's unity.

When at last he came to this touchy subject at the end of his letter, Paul named names. This was not done to expose the two, nor to hold them up to scorn before the rest of the church, but to make conjecturing unnecessary. When we rebuke sins or sinners with vague generalities, the persons in question are less likely to be convicted of sin or experience any healing. Instead, we may be doing the devil a favor by feeding gossip and erroneous speculation, thus alienating the contestants even more.

3. Be a mediator, not a judge. Though he called the two by name, Paul spoke in such compassion that he appeared neither censorious nor vindictive. There is an important principle here: If what we say is said in an obvious spirit of love, we may speak strongly without risking alienation. It is true that "wounds from a friend can be trusted" (Prov 27:6).

It seems significant, too, that Paul didn't take sides. Was he merely being tactful? Did he fear being caught in the middle, like an innocent bystander in a shoot-out between cops and robbers, or a boxing referee who finds himself absorbing punches meant for the contestants? Perhaps he felt too far removed from the situation to take sides with any degree of justice. Or maybe he knew that when two Christians come into conflict, the blame seldom rests exclusively on one of the adversaries.

Had Paul taken sides here, he easily might have further polarized the two women—and the church as well. An additional conflict (that is, over whether or not the apostle was just in his judgments) would have complicated the situation even more. So Paul addressed the two women evenhandedly: "I plead with Euodia and I plead with Syntyche . . ." (Phil 4:2). No partiality was shown. The idea was not to assign blame for the origin of the conflict but to show that both Euodia and Syntyche were mutually responsible to seek reconciliation and find a peaceful solution.

In any dispute, the fact that neither participant is likely to be without some blame ought to make us very slow to pass judgment, especially when the full facts of the case are not completely known to us.

It took me many years of experience in pastoral counseling before I really learned that lesson. When Ted and Frances, the first couple that I married, came to me facing the imminent dissolution of their marriage, I listened with what I thought was great patience to their bitter recriminations against each other. Then, thinking that I'd listened long enough to be able to assess the case fairly, I decided that the major blame for the breakdown of their marriage lay with Ted. I began to counsel the warring pair, clearly revealing my partisanship.

It was obvious almost from the start that I wasn't being very helpful. I was deeply discouraged at my apparent inability to aid them, but I charged Ted with stubbornness in refusing to hear what I was saying to him. In retrospect, I realize that I made Ted the scapegoat for my own failure as a peacemaker. In forming a relatively hasty judgment of the problem and pointing the finger of blame at just one party, I disqualified myself for the ministry of reconciliation that was so needed.

Paul made no such mistake in dealing with these two women. He didn't risk a hasty judgment, which inevitably leads to injustice. Paul was not merely tactful here. He knew he could not assess the situation from a distance, nor did he feel that laying the blame for the disagreement at the doorstep of either woman should be the point. The main point was to encourage both of them to seek reconciliation with each other, because their alienation from one another was not pleasing to God, whom they professed to serve. Paul was acting as a mediator, not a judge.

4. *Give praise before blame.* But Paul did more than withhold blame here: he actually had a word of praise for both feuding women! "These women . . . have contended at my side in the cause of the gospel . . ." (Phil 4:3). Euodia and Syntyche were sig-

nificant co-workers of Paul, and he acknowledged their contribution to the work of the kingdom. He followed the same approach he had used with the Philippian church as a whole: praise before blame.

Once again, this was not merely a psychological ploy aimed to put them in a good frame of mind before he exhorted them to make up their differences. Rather, the apostle showed once more the gift of appreciation for his fellow workers, a gift that characterized his ministry. His letters to the churches were studded with the names of individual saints whose work he commended. No service for Christ was too small to catch his eye; any evidence of devotion to the Lord evoked his admiration. This man was not a "loner"; he knew that his effectiveness as a servant of Christ depended in large measure on the teamwork of his colleagues. He knew he was indebted to them, and he never hesitated to say so.

In contrast, many of us seem to keep our appreciation for our co-workers to ourselves. We know their value, we sense their helpfulness to our ministry—but we seldom express our gratitude to them. We're especially silent in this regard when, for some reason or other, they've become a problem to us. We readily focus on their faults and quickly forget their virtues. Or, worse yet, we are vocal about their failures, and silent about their contributions.

How many marriages, friendships and Christian enterprises might have been saved if we had been quicker to express appreciation than judgment! Perhaps the Spirit of God is calling your attention to this passage, not only to prepare you to mediate between a present-day Euodia and a contemporary Syntyche someday. Perhaps he wants to reawaken within you a deep appreciation for your Christian brothers and sisters and to move you to express that appreciation without delay. It is a spiritual discipline worth cultivating to praise sincerely those we disagree with, even before we question them about their alleged failures.

In recent years, it has been my joy to serve in a church whose members are quick to express appreciation for one another. The atmosphere is not sticky with effusive tributes. Rather, there is a sweet smell of genuine thanksgiving for what church members see of Christ in one another: "Thank you for calling me to see how I'm doing. I felt so encouraged!" "We appreciate the good care you give to the nursery. We feel so confident leaving Jessica here!" "Your message really spoke to me. Thank you." Appreciation is an expression of the loving fellowship we enjoy and our gratitude for our fellow servants in the cause of Christ. When people are appreciated, they are encouraged to give their best in the Lord's work and to be open to any loving criticism which may need to be expressed.

Euodia and Syntyche may have been at sword's point, but Paul did not allow himself or his readers to forget that "these women . . . have contended at my side in the cause of the gospel." And he didn't call their faith into question or cast suspicion on the fruitfulness of their past service to Christ, just because they were currently at odds with each other. Along with the others, they were those "whose names are in the book of life" (Phil 4:3).

Why, then, are we so shocked when Christians clash? Why do we so quickly question their faith or motivation, instead of appreciating their labor for Christ? We need to remember how powerful the Enemy is and how vulnerable we all are to his attacks.

5. Place responsibility where it belongs. Paul placed the responsibility for reconciliation squarely (and equally) on both women. He didn't ask them to give up their individuality—the differences in their backgrounds and psychological make-ups naturally caused them to see some issues differently. But because Euodia was "in the Lord" and Syntyche was "in the Lord," he urged them to find their higher unity in Christ. Madeleine L'Engle aptly spoke of the need for such unity in her book, *Walking on Water,* when she reminded an interviewer, "I have a point of view. You have a point of view. But *God* has *view!*"

Paul didn't pretend that such unity comes easily to strongly opinionated people, but he indicated that it is possible. He asserted that such an agreement was the will of God for these two.

But how should they go about the task of finding their agreement in the Lord? The apostle didn't answer that question fully here, perhaps because he knew that Christ's teaching shed strong light on it, or because he was sure that the Spirit of God would enable them to find unity if they really longed for reconciliation.

But certainly there are some steps we as peacemakers can suggest to people in conflict:

A first step would be to admit that their present impasse cannot be the will of God for their relationship. By mentioning the disagreement between Euodia and Syntyche in a letter addressed to the whole church, Paul indicated that their difficulty with one another was affecting not only themselves but the entire congregation as well.

If we are to be peacemakers, we need to help each other face the same solemn truth. To recognize that disharmony with each other affects the health of the church will not automatically solve the problem, but it can be the first step in finding God's way out of a morass in which we allow ourselves to be entrapped. And it's not necessary to allocate blame before taking this first step. Either party to the conflict may recognize that the situation is intolerable, regardless of which one is chiefly responsible. Obviously it's better if both of the disputants recognize that the status quo is unbearable, but even if only one does, a start can be made toward settlement.

A second step we can suggest as peacemakers is for one or both parties to admit that, if they are to be reconciled, they'll need more wisdom than they presently possess. If they admit this, encourage them to ask God for the wisdom they lack, claiming the promise in James: "If any of you lacks wisdom, he should ask God, who gives generously to all without finding fault, and it will be given to him" (1:5-6). And if today's Euodia and Syntyche both recognize their lack of wisdom, they may be willing to learn to listen to each other in a new way, to stop hurling charges and countercharges at each other, and to see the whole picture more clearly than either has seen it before.

To do this, each will need the calming, discerning ministry of the Holy Spirit, who alone can bring them to the unity which the Lord desires for them. Martin Luther's hymn, "Rejoice in the Lord," would make an appropriate prayer:

Spirit, by Christ's atonement given,

to bring together earth and heaven,

in us, between us, silence strife,

and lead us out of death to life.

Agreement in the Lord is a mutual responsibility. As peacemakers we cannot force two people to reconcile. We must help them accept responsibility for seeking resolution in the power of the Spirit. As peacemakers, we can shine light on the path that needs to be taken: the need to admit that the conflict is intolerable to God and affects the unity of the church, and the need to ask God for wisdom larger than themselves in order to find resolution.

6. Bring in a third party. Let's be very practical: sometimes the clash between two Christians is at such an impasse that a third party is needed to assist in resolving the conflict. Paul could counsel these women from afar, but a third party on the scene was also needed: "I ask you, loyal yokefellow, help these women . . ." (Phil 4:3). This may have placed a heavy responsibility on the "yokefellow," but it was completely in line with Paul's teaching elsewhere that when a brother or sister is "caught in a sin," other believers have a responsibility to help restore them (Gal 6:1).

It's worth noting that when Paul asked a third party to intervene as mediator, he didn't try to tell him how to handle the case. He allowed the intermediary who was on the scene to decide how best to work out the problem with those most directly involved in it, all the while trusting the Lord for a happy solution. The reconciler was given space to devise the needed steps, rather than having to employ a particular method imposed upon him from outside. The apostle no doubt knew the folly of stereotyped approaches to such a sensitive matter, especially if they were devised by an absentee who lacked firsthand knowledge of a complex situation.

In calling a "loyal yokefellow" to share the task of peacemaking, Paul did not offer him an easy or pleasant task, or one without personal risk. The same is true for a peacemaker in the church today. Both parties in a conflict may be convinced that they are waging righteous warfare and give the strongest possible statements to their opinions. The person who steps in to try to mediate the dispute may find the role of peacemaker a rather dangerous one, with his or her own share of wounds as part of the price for intervening.

But for what greater ministry could a believer take risks than helping Christians once again find their unity in Christ? Surely the ministry of reconciliation is our high calling—and high privilege—as servants of the Lord Jesus: helping adversaries to hear each other more clearly, understand one another's views more fully and respond to each other in love instead of bitter animosity.

The true peacemaker, one who helps bridge the chasm of conflict, is a Christlike figure indeed. Such people will be called the children of God, for in the ministry of reconciliation, they manifest a family relationship to the heavenly Father. It is a ministry for angels—or for ordinary people like you and me who are willing to pay the price of being God's reconciling agents.

7. Be sensitive. It seems significant that Paul didn't go into any detail concerning the origin or nature of this quarrel. It's altogether possible that the little Christian community at Philippi was so aware of the cause of the quarrel that there was no need to repeat it. But there may be at least two other reasons for Paul's restraint.

He may have withheld the details out of loving concern for his two battle-weary friends. Paul decided it wasn't necessary to air the painful details to bring the women to grips with the situation, and to do so might have hurt their future relations within the church. Such details, if they needed restating, could be handled in a private letter. Paul's loving purpose was to help these two women, not to expose them further. He had felt compelled to allude to the conflict in his letter—as a true friend of these co-workers or the church itself, he had to do so. But Paul used discernment as to just how much needed to be said.

Besides, by ignoring the details of the quarrel, the apostle emphasized that reconciliation was the issue, not the quarrel itself. Had he stated the cause of the conflict, the Philippian church (and later generations) might have decided that the need to settle differences applied only in similar situations. This is certainly not the case, in Paul's day or in ours!

From century to century, there is a certain universality about the disagreements among Christians; it seems as if only the details differ. The apostle James asked, "What causes fights and quarrels among you?" (Jas 4:1). He then proceeded to answer his own question, recognizing the universal element underlying conflicts between Christians: the civil war that rages within us between our old and new natures, regardless of the particular spark that sets it off.

Remember . . .
I like to have the loose ends gathered up by the time a story is over.

But real life isn't always that neat! In more than one biblical story, we are left to wonder how the solution worked out. Even though we might like to know the early church's track record in conflict management, it is more helpful to understand how these Spirit-filled believers dealt with their conflicts.

In speaking directly to Euodia and Syntyche, Paul drove home the importance of being a peacemaker—and creating a positive context for peacemaking to take place. He didn't focus solely on the problem. He acknowledged the faith and fruitfulness of the persons involved—but he didn't beat around the bush, either. He didn't take sides. He placed responsibility for finding a resolution on both parties in the conflict. And he encouraged a third party close to the situation to take the risk of mediating the dispute.

Peacemaking is risky. It may mean throwing down your arms so that another will join you in peace talks. It may mean walking unarmed and unprotected onto another couple's battlefield. But, even though it is risky, Jesus promised, "Blessed are the peacemakers, for they will be called children of God."

11

It Will Take a Miracle!

I CAN ALMOST HEAR some of the responses to this book already.

"Dr. Fenton, what you've said in your book is encouraging and all that. But you don't know the struggle I'm experiencing. None of the conflicts that you've portrayed describe my situation. The rift is so long-standing! The feelings are so deep! The issues are so complex! It would take a miracle to resolve the problem I'm concerned about, and I see no hope of one!"

As any author might who shares a concern heavy on his heart, I find myself longing—and daring to hope—that this book *will* be helpful to some Christians who are struggling with the anguish of broken relationships. However, I fully realize that there may be negative reactions from readers whose high hopes for *the* Christian answer to conflict management were not rewarded.

Maybe you feel let down because the case studies—biblical or contemporary—do not seem to have relevance to your own desperate situation. Or you may feel that the types of healing cited do not offer a solution to your own relationship problems. If this is your response to this book, I want to hear it. I want to be sensitive to the pain you feel. I pray to God that I will continue to learn how to be more helpful whenever I address this subject.

On the other hand, I will not really be surprised if some readers are disappointed for the reasons cited above. The Bible is replete with people who felt that their situation was beyond solution, especially when no miracle of relief was immediately evident. In most cases, God was not asking too much faith of them. Usually, they had failed to recall the other harried souls who, like them, found fresh hope as the Lord revealed himself as a miracle-working God.

Moses, Jeremiah, the Apostles and You

There was Moses, for example, feeling burdened with a responsibility he felt incapable of carrying—leading God's people through a massive escape and an arduous journey to the Promised Land. When God personally appointed him, Moses was overwhelmed by the thought of the task and the qualifications he lacked. He exclaimed, "But that would take a miracle!"

He was right, of course: that's exactly what the job required. But he was wrong to assume that would make the task impossible, not only for him, but for an almighty God working through him. (See Ex 3:7-12 and 4:1, 10.) Moses sounded strangely like many of us when we face being peacemakers in a difficult situation. His words (and ours when they express a similar complaint) were not so much an indication of humility as a confession of unbelief.

Then there was Jeremiah. When God spoke to him, appointing him to be a prophet to the nations, Jeremiah objected, "I do not know how to speak; I am only a child" (Jer 1:6). Maybe Jeremiah had an idea how people would react to his attempts to reconcile them to God. Indeed, he was threatened with death, unjustly accused of treason, thrown in prison and even put into a well to starve to death! He faced a task that seemed totally beyond him, and he protested to God that he was young and inexperienced—and not a miracle worker! But God just said, "Do not be afraid of them, for I am with you and will rescue you" (Jer 1:8).

Look at the despair which gripped the disciples when Christ casually suggested they feed the hungry multitude. They cried out in dismay, sure of two things: It would take a miracle and there was little or no chance a miracle would take place (see Jn 6:5-9). Had I been among them that day, I probably would have reacted with the same disbelief. (After all, imagine it: fifty-five thousand fans at a baseball stadium and the refreshment stand having only two hot dogs and five hot-dog buns!)

You may be struggling with despair over a seemingly impossible conflict. You may honestly doubt that God can or will work a miracle in a shattered relationship. If so, you are not so unlike these very human biblical figures. You may not want to challenge the biblical record or the case studies I have cited, but it may be hard to find in them any hope for the bitter estrangement you face. I am sure your doubts are sincere and your hopelessness based on an inner pain you live with day after day. But I pray I can show you a reason you can hope again.

Grounds for Hope

The Bible doesn't mock us by offering sure-fire formulas for peace-making in our everyday relationships. (If your situation is X, do Y, and the result will be Z.) We have no God-given guarantee that success will always come to our efforts to restore harmony. We had better admit that.

But, as Christians, should we just throw our hands up, saying "I give up! I don't care anymore!"? I don't think so. Let us find some common ground on which to build hope.

1. Each situation is unique. There is a sense in which each individual battle is unique. There is no such thing as a standard situation which a universal formula will solve. No biblical incident, no experience of God's people down through the centuries, exactly parallels the tragic experience which keeps you awake at night and burdens your day. Even "similar" situations will be variously affected by the different personalities involved.

But admitting each situation is different does not mean one is so unique that nothing anyone else has learned or experienced applies. Rather, each situation shares the common ground of its own uniqueness. There may be much you can learn from other situations.

2. All relationship conflicts seem hopeless. The incidents of healed relationships cited in this book all have shared at least one experience: as the participants originally faced the problem, the situation seemed utterly hopeless. Each one had its own reason for appearing to be an irreparable rending of the fabric of human relations. You are not alone in your feelings of hopelessness; let's confess that in some measure all of us share that sense of dark despair when confronted with failed relationships. Take hope in the fact that your feeling may not be prophetic!

3. All relationship conflicts require God's help. Think about it. Didn't each incident that we have explored demand, and get, God's intervention in its solution? In each incident there seemed no way out, at least until God moved in ways that were seldom foreseen. Moreover, the reason that no panacea would work in these situations—or in yours—is that help seldom comes to us in our times of desperation until all human hope of a solution has fled!

One of my favorite chapters in the Bible is Acts 27, the story of

Paul's shipwreck and deliverance. The prisoner Paul was being sent to Rome by ship. After being battered by wind and waves "of hurricane force" for two weeks, everyone on board had lost all hope. Everyone—not just the pagan sailors, but Paul and Luke as well. Luke himself testified, *"We* finally gave up all hope of being saved" (Acts 27:20). Indeed, an angel of God had to exhort Paul to be of good courage (v. 24). Although the ship itself would be lost, the angel promised that "God has graciously given you the lives of all who sail with you" (v. 24).

We look to the same God to whom Paul turned in his hour of hopelessness and despair. In our relationship conflicts, we are dealing with the God who salvaged Paul's life and the lives of all who were with him, in spite of the raging elements of wind and storm. Our God delights in helping us in our hopelessness, not merely to sympathize with us, but to banish our despair by doing that which defies all human explanation— stilling the storms that rage in our churches, bringing light to dark situations, restoring lives and relationships we thought were lost.

So I want to say to readers who are dismayed by the sad state of their relationships, your situation may look beyond resolution, and surely it would be if it depended on your own effort. But like other "hopeless" situations, it can yet yield to the power of God!

4. A peaceful solution is *a miracle!* Of course it will take a miracle! Haven't we learned that that is true of every aspect of the Christian life? Only a miracle could help us live lives pleasing to a holy God. He asks from us an unselfishness that is impossible to attain in our own power. And God asks us to live lives of purity in a world of moral rottenness. Knowing our own hearts, we have to say, "No way, Lord—unless you work miracles in me day by day!"

To live at peace with each other is beyond our capability as well. To do so requires a miracle. There is no other way. Be willing to ask God for still another—in your conflicts.

5. Our God is a miracle-working God. Our God offers us the hope that he will indeed intervene in our tragic human situations. Such a miracle comes when we recognize the inadequacy of our own best efforts to bring peace to our troubled world. When we know that our human efforts to establish peace fall short, and couple our own sense of hopelessness with confidence in a God who helps the helpless, we can fix our hope where it should have been all the time—in a miracle-God. But we will have to pray Jehoshaphat's prayer: "We do not know what to do, but our eyes are upon you" (2 Chron 20:12). When we do, our God will move in to do what only he can do.

Latin America, as elsewhere, has been torn apart by long-standing conflicts between individuals, families and nations. Even bloody tribal warfare is not a thing of the past. Statesmen, psychiatrists, social workers and even Christian missionaries have thrown up their hands hopelessly, realizing how unlikely it is that this situation will ever change.

Certainly that would have been anyone's feeling who studied the relationship of two of the fiercest and most warlike tribes of Ecuador. The Jivaros (more recently known as the Shuar tribe) have long been known as cruel head-hunters, with a proud history of murderous conflict with the Achuar tribe. These two primitive groups were implacable enemies; there was little hope they would ever be reconciled. Faithful Christian missionaries working among them said, with an air of resignation verging on despair, "It would take a miracle!" And, of course, they were right.

But miracles still do happen in the midst of impossible situations, even in our nuclear age. Today, what seemed inconceivable in that hate-filled environment is coming to pass.

Less than a year ago, a group of Shuars and Achuars sat down together in the town of Makuma, Ecuador—not to arrange a truce, but to celebrate a measure of peace they were already experiencing. Two groups whose only contact had been intertribal hatred, aggression, torture and murder, came together in love, at a choral workshop, of all things! They wanted to learn how to sing the praises of the One who had brought peace, first to their individual hearts, and then to their relationships with each other! Their joyous reunion was made possible because they were new creatures in Christ, still far from perfect but already taught by the Spirit to love one another as brothers and sisters in Christ.

There is no adequate psychological explanation of how the change came to pass. It is beyond comprehension, unless one takes God into consideration. What was needed was a miracle, and that's what God did! It was not accomplished by applying some theory of conflict management, nor even by using a neat formula for handling such situations devised by an earnest student of the Word. No, this was God doing what only he can do, producing a "sign of the kingdom," foreshadowing the great day when the lion and the lamb shall feed together (see Is 11:6). What happened in Ecuador is a reminder that God is still in the business of doing miracles, building outposts of his peaceable kingdom where they never existed before.

I don't expect that many Christians will be able to identify readily with primitive, warlike tribes—except possibly in two respects. First, some of you may see in your own conflicts a situation no more hopeful than the one confronting these warriors for so long. Second, I dare to hope you will believe that the God who intervened in this circumstance will work for you in your relationships.

6. *We must ask forgiveness for our unbelief.* I have been rebuked in my own heart for having said, "It will take a miracle"—all the while doubting one would occur. God has had to forgive me time and time again for my unbelief. And while I may still have to admit that many Christian battles are hopeless apart from a miracle, I am

learning at the same time to rejoice, believing that God delights in redeeming "hopeless" situations.

My faith has been restored by studying the biblical incidents which I have shared in this book, and also by having seen with my own eyes how God can redeem tragic situations when Christians clash. I believe that warring Christians *can* be persuaded to lay down their arms, to admit their own responsibility for some part of the tragic situation and to reestablish loving relationships even after they had turned away in bitterness and despair.

I hope that many discouraged Christians will also be led to ask forgiveness for treating some conflicts as though they are beyond God's power. Do we believe our God can do what he says? Do we believe he has conquered sin and death? Do we believe God reconciles us to himself through the saving grace of Jesus Christ? Can we not then believe that God can reconcile us to one another?

7. Hear the witnesses speak. I believe that I am currently seeing such a victory by our almighty God. Many years ago a dedicated young pastor and his wife answered God's call to serve an inner-city church I admire. The work which Richard and Sara took up at Faith Church was often very discouraging. Urban renewal destroyed long-established neighborhoods; people were crowded, lonely, hostile; crime and vandalism created an atmosphere of fear and suspicion; young people with no vision for the future lived only for the day. But Richard and Sara sensed God telling them not to run away, but rather to trust him to bring a lighthouse into that sea of urban darkness.

The work was never easy, and the faith of both pastor and people was tested to the limit through the years. Humanly speaking there were no end to the good reasons for just walking away from what seemed an impossible assignment. The future of the ministry often looked dark, and it often appeared to be folly to carry on.

But Richard and Sara trusted a miracle-working God through many difficult years, and he delighted in vindicating their faith. Many in that dark area came to new life in Christ, their lives completely transformed by the gospel. The church's outreach grew; it had an impact on the community that most observers would not have dared to expect. Young people had their lives, as well as their souls, redeemed, and they went into the world to serve Christ. To paraphrase John's words, "The Light entered the urban darkness, and the darkness was not able to overcome it" (Jn 1:5).

And then—tragedy! What the Enemy was not able to accomplish from the outside, he accomplished by sowing seeds of bitter dissension within the band of believers. Whatever happened was obviously a masterstroke of Satan, and the consequences were predictable: accusations, grievances, estrangements, wounds painful beyond description; brothers and sisters in Christ no longer loving one another; the work hindered; the witness neutralized, if not altogether destroyed. It was a seemingly hopeless situation if ever there was one. My heart ached for Richard and Sara and their broken flock. Obviously a miracle was called for, but there was little hope that such an event was likely to take place.

But we who were weak in faith were dead wrong! I have no story of instantaneous change to report here. Even with miracles, the healing process usually takes time. But there is mounting evidence that God has moved into that painful conflict, that healing is taking place and unity is being restored.

An excerpt from the recent report of the elders to the congregation gives witness:

Brothers and sisters in Jesus Christ, these past months have included many afflictions, trials, troubles, hurts, and great pain. To the praise of God, we are still here—bruised, aching, and battered, but God has given us astounding help. This is God's doing—most certainly not ours. He has used these rough times to change our trust from mere man (whether pastor, elders, deacons, or deaconesses) to God himself. . . . Throughout the history of our church we assumed that we were immune from many of the troubles that other churches experience.

We have been humbled before God in our pride and smugness. I believe that we are in a much more strategic place for ministering to others now. Those who have experienced hurts and wounds can be more compassionate in bringing comfort to others who are hurting. This is what God says to us in II Corinthians 1:3-4: "Blessed be the God of our Lord Jesus Christ, the Father of mercies and God of all comfort, who comforts us in all of our affliction, so that we may be able to comfort those in any affliction with the comfort with which we ourselves are comforted by God."

We believe that this is a time for the healing of hurts and wounds from these past months and for growth in our trust and care for one another.

And the Pastor's Report for the same period read:

The Board of Elders Report gives some of the details of God's great mercy in bringing healing into that suffering part of his body known as Faith Church. May we never forget any of his benefits, who has pardoned all our iniquities and who has healed all our diseases (Ps 103:2-3)! God's healing has included our own personal relationships with God and ourselves, and has included reconciliation, renewed trust, and more unselfish love for one another. Yet we live in a world that is continually afflicting us with hurts—the world is not a friend of God or his family. We also confess our awareness of the possibility of our own family-of-God members hurting one another. Thus we are determined that "healing" and "reconciliation" shall continue to be distinctive emphases of this new church year, and of those further years God's grace continues to give to us. But healing and reconciliation are not God's great goal for us as his Church, but only the means to the undistracted commitment of us, God's people, to our Triune God. . . .

But there are horizontal dimensions of this commitment— our commitment to one another. "Encourage one another day after day, as long as it is still called today, lest any one of you be hardened by the deceitfulness of sin . . . and let us consider how to stimulate one another to love and good deeds, not forsaking our own assembling together as is the habit of some, but encouraging one another, and all the more, as you see the day near" (Heb 3:13; 10:24–25).

Our commitment to Christ, his Church, and his Commission has not been as wholehearted during this past year as it ought to have been. God's healing and reconciliation among us have removed many distractions. Let us gratefully respond to him with the commitment of all of our hearts, and all of our souls, and all of our strength (Mark 12:30).

These excerpts from the Annual Report tell us that the situation at Faith Church was so desperate as to seem hopeless by human judgment; that nothing short of a miracle would enable reconciliation, healing and restored fruitfulness; and that such a miracle had indeed come!

I needed a witness like that to rebuke my own unbelief. And I suspect that many of the readers of this book need to hear it with me. We say we believe, and then once again we confront a situation that drives us to the brink of despair and unbelief.

The experience of Faith Church says no more to me than the incidents from Scripture throughout this book. But the contemporary nature of this particular inner–city church's situation confirms the witness of the biblical accounts and reminds us that we have a God who helps those who can't help themselves—yes, even in our day.

Remember . . .

These records from church history—ancient and modern—may seem to portray conflicts very different from our own civil wars, but fundamentally they all have this in common: they represent desperate situations where the power of God can make a miraculous difference.

We dare not, then, give up hope. Our confidence must be based, not on techniques of conflict management (although we may learn much from them), but on the assurance that God wills the powerful witness of unity of all who love him. The process of peacemaking may be long and drawn out. The cost may be high—including death to our pride and to some of our long-cherished viewpoints, which we may easily mistake for God-given convictions. But with a sovereign God, all things are possible—even the miracle of reconciliation.